CRITERION FOR THE CHURCH

CRITERION FOR THE CHURCH

by

J. ROBERT NELSON

ABINGDON PRESS

NEW YORK   NASHVILLE

PRINTED AND BOUND IN ENGLAND BY
HAZELL WATSON AND VINEY LTD
AYLESBURY, BUCKS

Contents

Dedicated
to my
DEAR WIFE

Prologue

A VERY provocative thesis has been advanced by Professor J. C. Hoekendijk of Holland. In this time of heightened interest in the Church as a divine-human society, he claims that it is a sure sign of weakness in faith whenever Christians take much time to deliberate about the nature of the Church. Church members ought to be too busy with the mission of the Gospel to permit themselves the luxury of wondering what the Church is, he claims. *Do* what is required and let the *being* of the Church take care of itself!

There is truth, but not the whole truth, in his view. The Church is more than an activity in history. It has a distinctive form and a particular kind of corporate life, in addition to its mandated activity of service and mission. Obviously any church body which is preoccupied with itself, ceaselessly contemplating its image in a mirror in order to understand what it really is, is a defective church. It is doomed to answer to the description which a rural church in Tennessee inadvertently gave of itself when, for purposes of postal reduction, it actually stamped on its envelopes: 'A non-prophet organization.' But conversely, a church which has no regard at all for knowing its own nature can become engulfed, and finally exhausted, in its own activity.

The New Testament poses many questions and leaves most of them only partly answered. What is the Church? What must it do to be faithful? How should its life be lived? The answers are only pointed to, but not defined. So Christians today are increasingly disposed to return to the New Testament and reflect upon its witness in the light of past centuries of tradition and of present problems. In this they are discerning more clearly the lineaments of a local church which is both apostolic and contemporary, both consistent with the life and pattern of the earliest Christian community and yet vitally effective today.

In this book I have attempted to find concrete guidance for the present life of the Churches in the simple but very suggestive words of the Acts of the Apostles 2[42]. The four elements which are set forth there provide an admirable opportunity for discoursing on some of my chief concerns about the congregations of Christians now alive, and especially those of Protestant character in America. Although I began writing while teaching at Princeton Theological Seminary, I revised and concluded the book in India, during a year as visiting professor at Bangalore and Jabalpur. The distance from home did not diminish my concern for American churches; and new acquaintance with churches in this great Asian country gave me a more critical, detached perspective on the American scene.

The liberties which I have taken in drawing out the implications of this single text are cheerfully admitted, but no penitence is expressed on account of them. Neither do I feel embarrassed by the fact that the quadrilateral structure of the book permits no deliberate movement from preliminary problems and initial premises to logical conclusions.

Much of the material of these chapters was presented as the 1961 Peyton Lectures at Perkins School of Theology, Southern Methodist University in Dallas, Texas. Shorter portions were tried out on audiences of theological students and pastors at Westminster College in Salt Lake City, Moravian Theological Seminary in Bethlehem, Pennsylvania, and Carey College of Serampore, West Bengal. My sincere gratitude is here recorded to the officers of these institutions for their friendly courtesy and encouragement.

J. R. N.

OBERLIN, OHIO
September 1962

'And they devoted themselves . . .'

ONE

A Norm is Needed

I

IF WE CHRISTIANS are at all alert, we should know that we are past the time of easy existence in the world. The signs are evident, the voices are heard, and the books are at hand: all telling of the plight of the Church in the present day. It is true that Christians have always lived in some degree of crisis. The authentic existence of the Church in the world may at no time in history have been really easy. Whether living in peace or under persecution, whether as favoured majority or barely tolerated minority, Christians have known in every generation that some indispensable elements of their faith were in jeopardy and some features of the Church's work and witness were crippled by pre-vailing adversities. Whenever Christians are really true to their faith, they get into trouble with the world about them. When they are unfaithful to the truth of the Gospel on which the Church stands, they are in trouble with God.

When T. S. Eliot composed 'The Rock' as theology expressed in poetry, he wrote: 'The Church must be for ever building, for it is for ever decaying within and attacked from without.' Here he spoke perceptively of the double danger which has always threatened Christians. Such danger has been raised to a higher power today than ever before—within the Church: diluted faith, scepticism, unconcern for mission, perfunctory motion without meaning; outside the Church: disdain for God in lands where Christians are numerous, burst of population and outburst of ancient religions in lands where they are few. On these internal and external threats there is no need to dwell in this book. Our concern is not here to diagnose the ills of the Church nor to survey the unhealthful environment in which it now lives. The results of many competent studies in this area are well known. The diagnosis and analysis go on. But we know enough of the Church's plight already; enough, that is, to measure our task and seek resources for accomplishing it. It is wilful blindness to hard facts, rather than excusable ignorance of them, which prevents Christians from being sufficiently concerned for the integrity of the Gospel and the extension of the Church in the present time.

Instead of being emboldened by a clear perception of the signs of the times, many Christians are overwhelmed and intimidated. Despite their resolute continuance in Christian faith and worship, they feel within themselves the dark presentiment that the melancholy prophets and sharp-tongued adversaries are right. The Church is living on borrowed time, they feel. It is in the twilight which precedes its being swallowed by darkness. The growing opposition seems monstrous in size and mordant in hostility; but the Church's resources seem small and uncertain. If Christianity is to have any future at all, they concede, is it not best to let it dissolve in a blend with other religions and ideologies, give up its distinctive claims, and become part of the universal, enlightened religion for a new age? So run the thoughts of contemporary craven Christians. Therefore they are pitiable persons—not because they lack enough bravado to keep asserting the superiority and assured victory of the Christian religion in every context, but because they are unable to maintain real faith in Jesus Christ as the Lord to whom every knee shall bow.

At this time when every aspect of the Christian faith is endangered either by decay within the Church or attack from without, it may be helpful for each member to single out a particular issue and, holding it at arm's length, say: 'There is the crux of the crisis. There is our most clamant need.' Certainly such matters of faith, for example, as biblical authority, the incarnation and resurrection of Jesus Christ, and the personal reality of God are essential elements which require the utmost in clarity of thought and vigour of defence.

Yet we dare to propose that it is the Church itself which is the critical issue for the demonstration and defence of the truth of the Christian faith today. Among all living Christians, Bishop Stephen C. Neill has some of the widest knowledge and clearest vision of the present struggle of the faith in the world. Speaking of the peril of Christianity in the quicksands of Indian culture, he writes: 'The stumbling-block for the Hindu is the Church.'[1] The reason is that the Hindu, despite his involvement in his caste community, is entirely individualistic when he comes to apprehend his religion and express it in worship. Thus he cannot easily appreciate the Christian claim of the indispensability of the living community of faith and worship. But even if the Hindu could accept the Church as essential to religious faith, he is seldom impressed or attracted by the quality of the Church's life as he sees it externally in his society. And even if he could appraise the Church from the inside, as a sympathetic enquirer, it is dubious that many congregations would convincingly manifest the distinctive genius of the Church's life in its strength of faith, genuineness of personal community, worship and service.

Not only the Hindu, however, but the sceptical European or American has the same difficulty of learning what the Church is really intended to be. It is regrettable enough, from the Christian standpoint, that the people of society who bear Christ's name fail to manifest the true reality of the Church in their congregational life. But it is many times worse that Christians have no clear theological understanding of what the Church is and how its historical life should be formed in order to fulfil its elemental purposes.

Every person having even a modicum of information about contemporary theology knows of the formidable emphasis upon the concept of the Church.[2] In recent years it has been the pre-occupation of many Christian scholars to find a clearer understanding of both the essential nature of the Church and the

---

1. *Christian Faith and Other Faiths* (London: Oxford, 1961), p. 94.
2. See my survey of such studies between the years 1918 and 1948, *The Realm of Redemption* (London: Epworth Press, 1951; Greenwich: Seabury, 1951).

appropriate ways by which the churches should live in the world. The relevant biblical passages—and there are more than most people think—have been sifted and sorted and pondered in dozens of monographs. Library shelves have begun to sag under the weight of new books on the nature and function of the Church. Quite properly and purposefully there have been, and still are, theological study commissions at work on the meaning of the Church, under auspices of the councils of the ecumenical movement. The well-known phrase, 'Faith and Order', which designates so much of importance in this movement, means precisely the concern to know what the Church really is, as distinct from all our partial and distorted ideas of it.

It may be asserted ruefully that most pastors and church members are still virtually uninfluenced by this ecclesiological revival. Yet some who know the plethora of literature already feel that the theologians, like the folks of Kansas City in the song, 'have gone about as far as they can go'. As George W. Webber of the justly famous East Harlem Protestant Parish writes: 'One of the best ways to avoid living by the gospel is to spend time discussing the doctrine of the Church.'[3] And yet Webber has found in his distinctly difficult pastoral work a strong need for theological understanding of the Church.

After some twenty years or more of intensified interest in the nature of the Church we are in a position to see both the power and the impotence of the study of it. On the one hand, numerous Christians have found in a fresh doctrine of the Church the impetus to more vigorous thinking about what they believe, a more zealous mission to those outside the sphere of faith, and a more vital worship and common life within the Christian community. They have set out deliberately to shape and direct their own congregations according to best insights derived from biblical and theological study. Signs of church renewal resulting from such efforts are all about us. Some instances are well publicized; others are appropriately obscure. So in many places

3. *God's Colony in Man's World* (N.Y.: Abingdon, 1960), p. 42.

it is quite possible to discern a simple relation of cause and effect between the deepening theology of the Church and the manifestation of new life.

The impotence of the doctrine of the Church, on the other hand, is not only discernible in places but overwhelming to one who dreads seeing evidence of it. The theorem could readily be demonstrated that the vitality of the communal, liturgical and missionary spirit of the churches in certain lands or denominations is in inverse proportion to the profundity and comprehensiveness of the theology of the Church as taught in such places and churches. All of the intellectual force of the churchly theology of Karl Barth in Switzerland or of Bishops Aulén and Nygren in Sweden seems somehow to be at variance with the decrepit and declining life of churches in those lands. But lest we feel disposed to thank God, as did the pharisee in the temple, that our churches in America are not as others, let us be candid and honest enough to recognize the pitiful cleavage in our own country between the contemporary, vigorous theology of the Church and the actual infidelity and debility of many churches.

Obviously a neat theological definition of the Church is not sufficient to enable a congregation of lukewarm, poorly informed Christians really to be a living church. In a meeting of a theological commission on Faith and Order Professor Robert L. Calhoun had stressed the point that a true church must possess the classically defined elements of the Word, the Sacraments, order and discipline. Whereupon Professor Floyd V. Filson responded wryly that the church across the street from him had possessed all these—and still it died! The fault lay not in having these ecclesiastical marks, of course, but in having them in form rather than in force.

Whether with power or weakness, then, the emerging doctrine of the Church is being taught in theological seminaries today as never before. Less than twenty years ago, after I had completed the regular course of theological studies at a leading divinity school, no professor had even hinted to me that there was such a thing as a theological or doctrinal question about the Church. Had I then been questioned on the doctrine of the Church, I would have responded in the manner of those unnamed Ephesians who were asked whether they had received the Holy Spirit: I had never even heard that there was such a thing. But seminary curricula have changed radically since then. Today not many theological students can avoid hearing and learning a good deal about the Church. In most seminaries they learn that the Church is the instrument of God's choosing for effecting His purpose of salvation; that it is the Body of Christ of which He is the living Head; that it is a community of forgiven sinners convened for worship, mutual aid, and indiscriminate service; that it is universal and non-exclusive as to race and nationality and class; that the Church exists not for itself alone, but to glorify God and to carry out the mission of the Gospel to all mankind. Regardless of denominational and factional variations, these are the main elements of a doctrine of the Church which have wide currency in theological education today. They are not new discoveries about the Church, so much as recoveries of perennially valid knowledge which has for some generations been obscured.

But somehow these trenchant, dynamic ideas seldom come to expression in a pastor's own faith, preaching and teaching. They lie buried in forgotten class notes, or imprisoned in unread books, while the churches are allowed to continue in the ruts worn smooth by long usage. And as a result, a vigorous doctrine of the Church usually remains beyond the ken of most church members, who therefore never dream that there is anything essentially wrong or defective in the kind of conventional church life to which they are accustomed.

Despite certain evidence to the contrary, I cannot surrender the conviction that theology and practice are inseparable, and that a healthy church life depends to a very large degree upon a strong doctrine of the Church. This doctrine in turn derives from the apostolic witness and teaching of the New Testament.

As has been noted, our chief need today is not a critical diagnosis of the weakness, and even sickness, of many churches. The steady flow of such reports, even though not very cheerful, have been useful and helpful. So one is no longer considered a prophet when he declares that churches have succumbed to secular culture, that they are social clubs more than genuine communities, that they live for success rather than the Cross, that membership is too easy to attain and retain, that moral courage is lacking, that preaching sounds irrelevant, and that faith itself is generally vapid. All this we have heard and said. Our arms have grown weary in beating the ecclesiastical dead horses. The critics have not had to set up straw men, because churches themselves have stood self-exposed as stuffed with straw.

What began with the serious purpose of constructive criticism has unfortunately given way to a bitter, acid cynicism about the churches which is by no means constructive. This is no longer the attitude monopolized by the cultured despisers of Christianity. It belongs now to confessors of the faith, theological teachers and students, and not a few pastors. Some have simply concluded that the institutional forms of the Church are now beyond the possibility of salvaging for the sake of the Gospel. Better, they say, to go completely outside the organized churches to find the authentic Christian life. It is a good thing when Christians are self-critical and willing to examine the causes of the churches' malaise with both candour and the intention to reform. But the imperceptible boundary between criticism and cynicism is easily crossed. Some people are like awkward tourists bumbling across the border of, say, Czechoslovakia from West Germany. They are unaware that they have done so, until they recognize too late that their caustic words about the churches, fellow Christians and the Church are corroding both others and themselves, to the detriment of all.

The trouble with the incurably cynical critic of the Church is that he is not able to say positively what he wants to see in it. He is truly eloquent when, like a self-conscious Amos, he decries the weakness, distortion and irrelevance of the contemporary churches in America or elsewhere. But he seems to suffer from aphasia when one asks him for a description of a more valid and acceptable form of the Church. In extreme cases of such cynicism we are reminded of our Lord's fierce indictment of the pharisees, who neither enter the Kingdom of Heaven 'nor allow those who would enter to go in' (Mt 23[13]).

The responsible church critic is precisely the one who loves the Church, who is most concerned for its health and well-being, even when his words of castigation sound harsh. This kind of Christian critic joins the increasing numbers today who are striving to awaken dozing members to our common plight and to make way for genuine reformation and renewal. However much some may prize the achievements of the sixteenth-century Reformation, it does that great movement no credit to consider it a closed chapter in the story of the Church. The Reformation is not yet completed. For the universal Church as well as the local congregation is always to be reformed, *ecclesia semper reformanda*, as the Presbyterians rightly insist.

Reformation and renewal do not just happen by themselves, however. Nor can they be effected solely by hierarchical decrees or by stepped-up programmes of denominational advance. New life for the Church can come only from the Lord and giver of life, the Holy Spirit. And He works according to His own divine wisdom and power, which is a way of saying that He brings renewal through the continuous effect of the Word of God, incarnate in Jesus Christ, perceived and witnessed to by the apostles, and appropriated by the Church. When we deal with the idea of the Church in terms of Jesus Christ and the apostolic witness, however, we do not limit ourselves to a static situation in ancient times when Jesus of Nazareth and later some men called apostles did and said certain things. We are dealing also with the health, reformation and renewal of the Christian Church in the present day.

II

Much talk about reformation today, significant as it surely is, fails to be really helpful because of vagueness about a criterion of reform. Is there not some standard, some canon or pattern, by which the whole life-process of the historic Body of Christ can be measured? To be sure, we cannot hope for the metrical accuracy which science requires. But we need not for that reason lapse into a relativism which permits no criteria at all. Even the quality of 'sincerity', which for sentimental Christians seems to be an adequate ground for judging all religious convictions and practices, is better than none at all.

Without a criterion, it is impossible to say whether any change in the life of a church is a reformation or a deformation. A bishop in an Asian land, irritated by the unco-operative stiffness of the Dutch Reformed Church, referred to it in humour but with a sense of fitness as the 'Much Deformed Church'. No doubt he had his criterion. But which one would be normative and applicable to every church called Christian?

Obviously it is sufficient for the faith of many Christians to say that the supreme standard is the Holy Scriptures. Who would want to dispute this as a general statement? One need not be a biblical literalist nor even a conservative to affirm the Bible as the authoritative norm. But according to what interpretation? The Christians of the world are notoriously and inevitably divided among themselves on the exact meaning of biblical authority. On one extreme are those who find as tolerable in the Church only those practices, beliefs and institutions which are explicitly commended in the Bible. At the other pole are Christians who gladly permit anything which is neither repugnant to Scripture nor contrary to sound reason. These cannot be reconciled. Who is right? We all have our viewpoints on the question of veracity and authority. But it is evident that an appeal to the Bible in general, without any agreement on the mode or meaning of interpretation, cannot satisfy the need for a criterion of reformation in the faith and life of the Church.

But there is a criterion which is sufficiently specific and applicable to cover most of the needs of the Church. It does not oppose nor minimize biblical authority as such, but rather enhances it. It is the criterion of *apostolicity*.

Apostolicity is the exact opposite of apostasy. Between these two poles all churches continue their existence in history, now near one pole, now moving in the direction of the other.

By 'apostasy' we simply mean that standing-apart from the expression and affirmation of the Gospel of Jesus Christ, which makes a person or a community cease to merit the name Christian. It is an ugly and horrifying word for any faithful Christian. It may be applied to another only with the greatest care and trepidation. Yet its ugliness must not cause us to reject it from our vocabulary. Apostasy is a trap into which, but for the grace of God, any of us can easily fall. Just as the word 'truth' has meaning only in relation to its opposite, 'falsehood', so apostolicity is understood in contrast to the apostasy which threatens it.

'Apostolicity' requires today a more careful definition than it has had in recent theological usage. We may not reach the time when the whole Christian community will agree on a definition of it, especially because of its connotations in Eastern Orthodox and Western Catholic traditions. Therein the word generally means creeds, canons, and episcopal succession. To the Roman Catholics it means in addition, of course, the apostolic see, the chair occupied by Pope John XXIII. Yet it is to be hoped that Protestants will rise above ancestral prejudice and seek such understanding of the concept that it may be clearly recognized for its inherent worth as a criterion of faith and life. Just now it is not easy to say exactly what apostolicity means to most Protestants, especially those in America; but generally it connotes the *time* of the apostles and their achievements, and not much else. It is for them, at the most, an historical term rather than a normative theological one. Hence it is fair to say that most Protestant Christians, including the theologians, seldom ask whether the message they declare and teach, or the life of the Church as they experience it, is in accord with the principle of apostolicity.

The earliest account of the beginning of the Christian Church was written by St Luke the Evangelist and subsequently designated by the faithful as the Acts of the Apostles. Often today it is simply called 'Acts'. But it is no light thing to delete reference to the apostles. In this book the primary concern is God's saving presence and work in Jesus Christ; and God the Holy Spirit is acknowledged as the power behind the actions of the story. But the actors in this unrepeatable drama of the first Christian generation were the men called apostles. And whatsoever was true and right with the Church at that time was defined in terms of the experience of the apostles, their perception of the saving revelation of God in Jesus Christ, their witness to His life and work and risen presence, and their discriminating judgement with regard to what was legitimate and necessary for the nascent Church. Out of the witness of the apostles to the Lord came the traditions which were written as the Four Gospels. And out of their knowledge of Jesus Christ and their inspired reflection upon the meaning of His coming were written the New Testament letters which have given form and content to the Christian faith for all time.

Against the background of the Church's apostolic origin, and for reasons which will become clearer, we can project a working definition of the term in its simplest sense. *Apostolicity means faithful congruity to the teaching and message of the apostles, in such wise that unbroken continuity is maintained with the earthly life of Jesus Christ.* It is this which is commended as the constant standard for the Church.

Does this criterion of apostolicity, as seen in the New Testament, give us any indication of what the specific aspects of the Church's life should be? Yes, these are most pointedly desig-

nated in one passage especially, Acts of the Apostles 2^{42}. Here
were set forth the four main elements of the criterion of apostolicity. We read that the first members of the apostolic Church
'devoted themselves to the apostles' teaching and fellowship, to
the breaking of bread and the prayers'. These elements apply to
the Church both then and now, both as local congregation and
as universal community of faith in wider dimensions. They do
not define in fullness, however, what constitutes the apostolic
Church. They are four among several factors, which include as
well the Church's missionary extension, its works of loving service and reconciliation, and the ordering of its cultic and social
life according to the functions called ministries. But the four
things to which the Christians devoted themselves show us those
primary dimensions in which God, speaking through the apostles
of Jesus Christ, desires the Church to be continuously reformed
and renewed. And it may be expected confidently that a Christian congregation which really persists faithfully in the apostles'
teaching, fellowship, breaking of bread and prayers will also
fulfil its responsibilities in those other areas of activity which
belong to the Church's reason for existence on earth.

III

In the ecumenical movement of the present time, with its strong
emphasis upon the world-wide missionary task of the whole
Church, there has been increasing use of the word 'apostolicity'.
Here it is used to stress the fact that all Christians as members of
the Church are under obligation to be witnesses to the Gospel.
Woe is me if I preach not! should be thought and felt by every
Christian. The Church, then, is apostolic in this sense or it fails
to be its true self. No mission, no Church!

Without detracting from the great importance of this usage,
we need to keep in mind a referent of the word which is no less
significant. There is no satisfactory meaning of 'apostolicity'
without conscious reference to the men called apostles. To
many modern Christians this is not self-evidently true. Why the

apostles? they ask. Why are they and their teaching called essential and indispensable to the Church in all ages? To be sure, they are the venerated founding fathers of the Church. But have they not been superseded by saints and sages of later times, having interpretations of the faith more relevant to our day? Why dubious old Thomas, for example, when you can get the answers from Thomas Aquinas? Why Paul of Tarsus when you can hear and read Paul Tillich? Indeed, is not any Christian who effectively preaches and explains the Gospel as much a true apostle as those of the New Testament who are so designated? In his book on the ministry of St Paul, William Baird desires to show that an apostle is simply any man in any time who 'truly proclaims the gospel'.[4] There is a worthy intention behind this kind of definition. He seeks to hold up the supremacy of the Gospel and to keep human authority in its proper subordinate place, as well as to dignify the missionary activity of every Christian who attempts to share his faith with another. But the apparent intention and the conclusion which he draws do not quite square with the recorded evidence of the New Testament.

The apostles had a unique identity and a unique function. They were not all in the categories of religious genius, pious holy-man, theologian or eloquent preacher. Far from it! They were among the lowly and despised in society. It is unlikely that certain of the apostles, if they lived now, would rate a D.D. degree from the most backward college in the land. Despite these deficiencies of wit and ability, they had been given a unique and indelible character. It was due to their having accompanied the Lord Jesus and having known Him between the time of His baptism and ascension, as Peter is quoted in Acts of the Apostles 1[21], when the successor to Judas was being chosen. Of such credentials they could not be deprived. Nor could anyone bestow the apostolic identity upon another who lacked the experience of being an eye-witness of the Risen Lord. 'According to the united witness of the New Testament,' writes Oscar

4. *Paul's Message and Mission* (N.Y.: Abingdon, 1960), p. 98.

Cullmann in his book about Peter, 'the apostolic office, particularly that of the Twelve, is a unique office not to be repeated.'[5]

Because of their unique identity, the apostles had a singular vocation on behalf of the Church and of mankind. They were our historical links with the Person of Jesus Christ and the witnesses to His work. As Thomas F. Torrance graphically describes their role, 'the Apostles formed the *hinges* of the divine mission, where, so to speak, the vertical mission in the sending of the Son by the Father, is folded out horizontally into history at Pentecost'.[6] According to this metaphor, the apostles were literally the first 'cardinals' and their witness and teaching were the cardinal fact for the Christian faith, since the very being and integrity of the Church hinged upon the truth of it.

A similar understanding of the apostles' function has been expressed by Emil Brunner in a sentence which, perhaps unintentionally, has a double meaning: 'The Church comes into being only because the Apostle comes forth from his secret intercourse with God and turns to others, giving them in the third person what God Himself gave him in his heart in the second person.'[7] No doubt the eminent theologian of Zürich meant to say that after the apostle had been addressed personally as 'thou' by the Lord, he turned to others and told them in his witness who the Lord was and what He had done. Brunner's reference was to a grammatical distinction. But is not the same truth expressed if we think of the second and third persons, not as elements of grammar, but as the classic designations of the Trinity? From their personal relation with Jesus Christ the Son, the apostles turned to others and communicated to them through the enlightening agency of the Holy Spirit.

Despite Karl Barth's disagreement with Brunner on certain

5. *Peter: Disciple—Apostle—Martyr* (Philadelphia: Westminster, 1953; London: S.C.M., 1953), p. 215.

6. *Royal Priesthood* (Edinburgh: Oliver & Boyd, 1955), p. 27.

7. *Revelation and Reason* (Philadelphia: Westminster, 1946; London: S.C.M., 1947), p. 123.

theological issues, the two Swiss mentors to contemporary Protestant theology do agree on the basis of apostolicity. The apostles were 'the earthly-historical medium' between God known in Jesus Christ and all of mankind who have since then been able to know Him in faith. Barth continues by saying the apostles were 'those in whose midst He has lived on earth, in history, as the Word of God made flesh, those who have seen and heard and handled Him in the servant-form of His flesh, but also in His glory'.[8]

These writers are cited, not because of their infallibility, for such they do not possess, but because they give clear expression to the portrait of the apostles found in the New Testament. And it is in the light of this interpretation that we can understand what is meant in the Letter to the Ephesians that the Church, as the household of God, is 'built upon the foundation of the apostles and prophets, Christ Jesus himself being the chief cornerstone' (2^{20}). A building can have only one foundation. And no matter how the building may grow—the Church's members are *living* stones—or be remodelled, the unalterable shape is determined by the foundation. Some churches today, having left the proper foundation in the drift from apostolicity in the direction of apostasy, have become rather like castles in the air. They may have their uses, particularly in this incipient space age, but they have lost their tie to the earthly reality of God's redemptive work in Christ, of which the apostles were the irreplaceable witnesses.

If the peculiar function of the apostles was to be the historic links or hinges connecting Jesus Christ with the gathering community, the mode of fulfilling that function was primarily their proclamation and teaching of the new Gospel. As unique representatives of the Lord they exercised various other works in the economy of the Church. It was their calling and task to be the founders and initial leaders of new congregations throughout the Roman Empire and perhaps beyond it, as in the legend of

8. *Church Dogmatics* (Edinburgh: T. & T. Clark), IV. 1, p. 718.

Thomas in India. Their persistence in this task led invariably to their sharing in the sufferings of the Lord, that is, to their persecution and death as martyrs. For a time they were the men especially empowered by the Holy Spirit not only to preach but to heal and effect wondrous deeds as signs of God's immanent power. They were, moreover, the ones responsible for exercising discipline in the congregations, as Paul's letters clearly demonstrate. The apostles were the chosen leaders who first bound the churches together in a real manifestation of the unity which was the intention and gift of God to the Church. Lastly, whatever conclusions may be drawn with respect to the debatable origins of the ordained ministry and episcopacy, it is evident that the apostles had the authority to commission their fellow believers to be deacons and elders and general overseers of the churches. When we speak today of apostolicity in reference to the present churches, we do not ignore these continuing elements in the ordering of the Church's life which were initiated by the apostles.

It is deplorable that this last-named part of the apostles' role, having to do with ministry, has so dominated recent discussion of apostleship that it has driven from the stage all other apostolic functions. Just as excesses of Roman Catholic mariology have caused some Protestants to react negatively to the mere mention of the name of the Lord's mother, so the Catholics' insistence upon the apostolic succession has conditioned many to disregard the very authority of the apostolic office. What even many Catholics fail to notice, or perhaps to acknowledge, is that the concept of apostolic succession itself is patent of a variety of quite distinct meanings. These are held in good faith and with conviction by members of several communions. Edmund Schlink has sharply delineated at least five of them, as follows:

(1) The unbroken succession of bishops by the laying-on of hands as a formal principle of continuity with the apostles themselves.

(2) The same, but augmented by adherence to a definite body of doctrine and tradition.

(3) The unbroken succession of presbyters by the laying-on of hands of other presbyters.

(4) The continuity of apostolic doctrine, strengthened by the succession of the historic episcopate which is regarded as valuable but not indispensable to the Church.

(5) The continuity of apostolic doctrine in the life of the churches from generation to generation and the faithful preaching of the same.[9]

It is beyond the range both of this discussion and of presently discerned possibility to resolve all the intractable disagreements and church divisions which have existed for long years because of contrary views of apostolic succession. At least in current ecumenical studies and church union negotiations much of the acerbity, prejudice and misunderstanding are being removed. But the significant thing to underscore here is the fact that the diverse and divided churches which espouse any one of the five views are all concerned to honour faithfully and uncompromisingly the apostolic authority which is set forth in the New Testament.

IV

The apostles lived their allotted years during the first century, subject to the social and cultural conditioning of their time and place. So how, it is often asked, are we Christians able to recapture the life and character of the apostolic Church? The answer proposed by some Christians today is disarmingly simple: Let the Church take the form it had in the time of the apostles. This is appealing. There is a tendency among Christians to be inordinately sentimental about certain 'golden ages' of the Church's history. According to the varieties of their interest, they idealize the New Testament community, the Church of the

9. 'Die apostolische Sukzession' in *Kerygma und Dogma* (1961–2), p. 79.

first five centuries, the thirteenth century, the Church of the Reformation, the movement of the Wesleys, or the little brown church in the vale. But there is little practical help for the improving of church life today which can come from the indulging in sentimental thoughts about the churches of yesterday.

The Christians described in the Acts of the Apostles did not live in an ecclesiastical Garden of Eden. There was never a time when they could live in community with a shameless disregard for such metaphorical fig leaves as might cover the defects in their faith and service. Heaven may have lain about the Church in its infancy; but the clouds of glory which came trailing after did not long persist after the first few years. Not even in the days of the apostles could the Church be described as a colony of heaven which perfectly reflected on this planet the way of life in the homeland.

In calling for the renewal of the churches according to the criterion of apostolicity, therefore, we need not embrace the doctrinaire position of New Testament restorationism. There is a partial validity to this view in so far as it emphasizes precisely some basic elements for which we have been contending: namely, the normative truth of the apostolic message, the pristine sense of community, and the personal life of faith in Jesus Christ. But the unconvincing error of restorationism is its notion that the churches of the twentieth century can readily and exactly assume the form and character of the Church of the first century. The inevitably unsuccessful efforts to do this have led some Christians into a state of self-delusion and hypocrisy.

It is a further error of restorationism to reject the fruits of God's work through the Church in its history. The immeasurable composite of faithful worship, loving affection, courageous righteousness, and zealous mission is apparently lumped together with the well-known garbage of the churches' failures and sins, and nineteen centuries of the Holy Spirit's work is rejected as insignificant. It is true that this total carelessness about the history of the Church is the fault of extremists, and they are relatively few. But this observation is worth recording anyhow, because there is a bit of the delusion of extreme restorationism in most Protestants, and not only in certain members of the tribe of Alexander Campbell. Often we are tempted to a wistful, quixotic and ultimately insatiable nostalgia for the good old days of Acts of the Apostles 2.

Thus even the noted Reformed theologian, Emil Brunner, writing in *The Misunderstanding of the Church*, virtually deplores the human substance of the Church's history.[10] He despairs of finding true community in the contemporary churches and gazes back with longing towards the little community of the New Testament. Or else he finds manifestation of the pure community of the Spirit, not in any church, but outside the churches in voluntary groups of Christians. In latter years, since his famous visit to Japan as a visiting professor, Brunner has wholeheartedly endorsed the *Mukyokai*, or 'No-church Movement'. This is the group of very sincere Japanese Christians who have rejected and avoided any institutional form of the Church even more scrupulously than have the Society of Friends. It is this utterly non-institutional kind of corporate living which Brunner sees in the Church (*ekklesia*) of the New Testament. And this he would like to see restored in the present day as a substitute for any and every kind of institutional organization of the Church.

It is extremely optimistic to hold that the pattern of the New Testament Church can be exactly reproduced today. It is excessively pessimistic to consider the present-day churches as totally beyond the possibility of expressing the genius of the Church's community in their normal life. The evidence is unconvincing that either of these extreme views need be held. Rather, we can surely hold the median position that the Church and its constituent congregations are always reformable by the effective

10. (Philadelphia: Westminster, 1952; London: Lutterworth, 1952.) In his latest book Brunner expands this view—*The Christian Doctrine of the Church, Faith and the Consummation*, 1962.

power of the Holy Spirit. The acknowledged and deplored deficiencies of communal life and faith can be corrected by the same Spirit and according to the same criterion of the Church that was known and exemplified in the apostolic fellowship.

'. . . to the apostles' teaching . . .'

TWO

Bearing the Apostles' Message

BEFORE ALL else our chief concern is with what Christians believe and what they have to tell others which can make a lasting difference in the others' lives. The first believers in Jerusalem persisted obstinately in the teaching of the apostles. It was the apostles' teaching, their *didaché*, their witness to the incarnate Word of God whom they had known in Galilee and Golgotha and among the tombs—it was this apostolic message which attracted the earliest converts and accounted for their being drawn together in a new community of faith. It would be fruitless to debate with St Paul over his assertion that love is the greatest of the spiritual gifts to men; and one would not wish to be numbered among those who say that good works themselves, without faith, are dead. Nevertheless it is proper to point out that neither the loving example nor the charitable deeds of the apostles could possibly explain why some three thousand persons suddenly committed themselves in faith to Jesus Christ as Lord and thus embraced the new way of life.

Not the works, but the words of the apostles were the magnetic centre of the Church. For the words of their teaching and preaching told of the saving Person and of the happenings which marked the critical turning-point not only in the lives of the believers but of the whole human race. And as we scan the centuries of the Church's historical existence, the conclusion of the Heidelberg theologian, Peter Brunner, seems valid. He writes: 'The Church is apostolic in so far as it is sent into the world with the witness to Christ which began in the mouth of the apostles.'[1] And it is well worth considering that a congregation today can be authenticated as real church to the degree that

1. In *Oekumenische Rundschau*, IV. IV. (December 1955), p. 116.

its members devote themselves to the apostolic Gospel of the same Christ. As Carl Michalson declares: 'The history of the living church is the history of the will to maintain continuity with the apostolic witness. When one is called to witness to the gospel, he is called into a community of interpretation which presupposes an entire history of Christian witness.'[2]

While the debate about ministerial succession goes on, as it must for many more years, we may stress the conviction that apostolicity inheres primarily in the message of salvation which the apostles knew and proclaimed on the basis of their knowledge of Jesus Christ. The pedigree of preaching is a matter nearer the centre of apostolicity than the breeding of bishops. Or, conversely, the distance from the apostles is more readily seen in the anaemic faith and teaching of many contemporary churches than in their well-preserved order and ministry.

The trap into which we are easily tempted to fall these days is that of regarding the Gospel as a body of general religious knowledge or a code of religious principles which, with only the slightest mental and moral effort, can be followed in the routine of living. Certainly this is the vulgarized, common-sense, men's club and family magazine version of the Christian faith. And not much of our Sunday morning preaching or adult class teaching serves to correct this gross distortion. Old Pelagius himself would fly to the arms of St Augustine and beg forgiveness if he could hear some of the versions of the Gospel which are popularly held and taught today. There is a common-sense credo, currently confessed in the churches, which if analysed would yield such conventional thoughts as these:

Jesus of Nazareth was either a man of peerless morality, or else a divine emissary from heaven who tells us that the world is a very bad place in which to live.

The essence of Christianity is to do good for its own sake.

The value of the Bible is that it provides a steady philosophy of life.

2. *The Hinge of History* (N.Y.: Scribner's, 1959), p. 228.

Truth in religion is a fine thing, so long as no group really claims
to know it.

Man's urgent need is to put his mind at ease and enjoy unruffled
mental hygiene.

The Church is a good influence in society, like the home and the
school.

The basis of mission is to be kind to other people.

The Christian recommendation for social ethics is that everyone
ought to obey the laws of the State.

The destiny of man will be fulfilled in a righteous social order—
or as latter-day pseudo-eschatology tells us, in human extinc-
tion by atomic fission.

Let not your heart be troubled, however, because the soul is
surely immortal and so there need be no fear.

If I be accused of caricaturing the state of such thinking among
the members of most churches, especially in America, I willingly
plead guilty. No effective cartoonist would surrender his right to
caricature in expressing what he sees, for in this way he can depict
the truth more forcefully. And the appropriate response to this
spate of degenerate Christian teaching is not to stop the ears and
tear at the suit one happens to be wearing, as blasphemy was
greeted in days of yore. The response is to ponder afresh the
nature of the apostolic message, and to wrestle with the urgent
problem of how to commend Jesus Christ and His Gospel to an
evil and adulterous—and terribly bewildered—generation.

It is easy enough to assert that the apostolic message is the
core of the Christian faith, and thus the criterion for our teaching,
preaching and believing in this and every century. But how are
we to understand the content of that message?

Those who have read any theology at all during the past
twenty-five years know that the Greek New Testament's word
for proclamation, kérygma, has been the object of intensive
examination. It was in 1936 that C. H. Dodd's slender but significant book, *The Apostolic Preaching and Its Developments*,

appeared.[3] It has been a salutary thing for Christianity today that the nature of the kérygma has been studied exactingly. Thanks to the work of competent biblical scholars, we are now enabled to perceive more clearly the ingredients of the apostolic faith. And this has given rise to the kerygmatic theology of our day. But unhappily, and perhaps inevitably, the word kérygma itself has become so commonplace and such a cliché that there has been more cheering for the idea of a message to be preached than serious clarifying of what should be preached today which is congruous with the apostolic message and intelligible to people whose minds do not work in biblical categories.

'It pleased God through the folly of the kérygma to save those who believe,' wrote the Apostle Paul (1 Cor. 1[21]). He should have known this well enough, for he was unrivalled as the chief herald of the Gospel to the world. But just exactly what was preached by the apostles? The substance of the message is as familiar to the students of the Bible as it is still foolishness to the pretentious wisdom of the world. When the apostles turned from their communion with Jesus Christ to address their fellow mortals, they proclaimed the news of salvation as follows:

The long period of man's longing and of Israel's expectation had come to an end, and the new age of fulfilment had dawned.

This tremendous and incomparable change in man's history and his relation to God the Creator had come about because of the ministry, the death on the Cross, and the resurrection of Jesus the Christ. His coming as Messiah-King and Deliverer from sin and death was in accord with the expectation of the Scriptures of Israel.

In being raised from the dead on the third day, Jesus was exalted

3. (London: Hodder & Stoughton, 1936; 2nd edn, 1944, pp. 21–4.) Support for Dodd's interpretation is given by Floyd V. Filson, *Jesus Christ the Risen Lord* (N.Y.: Abingdon, 1956), pp. 41–54; Bo Reicke, 'A Synopsis of Early Christian Preaching', in *The Root of the Vine*, edited by A. Fridrichsen (London: A. & C. Black, 1953; N.Y.: Philosophical Library, 1953), pp. 139–42; and P.-H. Menoud, *La vie de l'Eglise naissante* (Neuchâtel et Paris: Delachaux et Niestlé, 1952), **p. 15.**

to the 'right hand of God' and made Lord over the Church and the world.

Thereupon the Holy Spirit of God had been given in power to the Church, to guide it in its life and mission until the consummation of the Reign of God in the final coming of Jesus Christ.

In response to this proclamation, people were called upon to believe in Jesus Christ, to repent of their sins, be baptized, and become members of the redeemed community, the Church.

This was the Gospel as first preached in Jerusalem to the Jews. When Paul and others carried the message to the Greeks, they did not change it in substance but had to speak of the one true God as the primal object of faith, from whom the Gospel of Jesus Christ was derived.[4] But whether addressed to Jew or Gentile, the apostolic message was simply an outthrust index finger pointing to Jesus Christ. None of the dialectic, exhortation, reassurance, threatening, bargaining or calculated rhetoric which have characterized much Christian preaching through the centuries. Just a stark assertion of the joyously incredible fact that He who is the ultimate Lord of all life had been revealed to men, crucified as a real man among them, and raised from the cold grip of death.

But wait a minute! Is there not some confusion of terms here? We suggested above that Acts of the Apostles 2[42] was a basic statement of the pattern of apostolicity for the Church. It is written there that the earliest Christians devoted themselves to the apostles' teaching, the *didaché* in Greek. But now we have been discussing the apostles' preaching or proclamation, *kérygma*. Are these the same or are they different from one another? The answer is not self-evident, so there is room for discussion. C. H. Dodd drew a rather clear distinction between them. In his view, the *kérygma* was just the commanding announcement by the apostolic 'town crier' that Jesus the Christ

4. This point is well made by Rudolf Bultmann, *Theology of the New Testament* (N.Y.: Scribner's, 1951; London: S.C.M., 1952), I. p. 65.

had come, been killed and raised from the dead. When people heard this and felt constrained to believe it, as multitudes did, they were then introduced to the religious and moral tenets of the new faith by being taught the didaché. Such was the origin of Christian education. Now to make this distinction does seem to make sense. There is a way of addressing the people outside the Church and a way of instructing those who have voluntarily come within it. But in drawing so bald a distinction between kérygma and didaché as to their content, Dodd made himself vulnerable to criticism. Can this kind of separation really be found in the New Testament? Jesus Himself, after all, was known equally as preacher and teacher. It would be quite artificial and unwarranted to distinguish His preaching of the coming Reign of God from His teaching of the ethical dimensions of life in this realm. Each of the four gospels written about Him is at least as kerygmatic as it is didactic. And in Acts of the Apostles 5, where it is told how the apostles Peter and John ran foul of the law because they were 'teaching' in public, it is a plain fact that they were preaching the Gospel. So it is more than an academic dispute when Gustaf Wingren rightly criticizes Dodd's distinction as a 'false intellectualism' and asserts that the essential content of kérygma and didaché is the same, namely, the crucified and risen Lord Jesus Christ.[5]

What does all this mean? Is it just the sport of splitting biblical hairs by the heirs of differing schools? Is it just a return to the familiar and sterile debate between the religion of Jesus and the religion about Jesus? Not at all! This serious struggle to identify the content of the apostolic preaching and teaching is motivated by the scholars' own sense of need to strip the Christian message of needless and encumbering accretions so that it may be advanced more effectively in each time and place. The scholar's study, the classroom, the printing press, the radio and television, the pulpit and the coffee table are all in the

5. *The Living Word* (Philadelphia: Muhlenburg, 1960), p. 18. Also Floyd V. Filson, *Jesus Christ the Risen Lord*, p. 34.

service of the one and the same Gospel. Whoever the hearer and speaker, and whatever the mode of communication, the pristine message which the apostles have bequeathed to the Church is without alteration in substance or diminution of power. And the measure of the apostolicity of a church is the degree to which it adheres to the Gospel, lives by it, and endeavours to share it with that growing majority of the human population which does not even know of Jesus Christ as yet.

Easily said. But in these days of revolution and accelerated secularization of man's thinking is there really any hope that the ancient apostolic message can still be proclaimed, taught, understood and accepted? Even if Rudolf Bultmann had never written a sentence, we would scarcely need to be reminded that the incarnation and death of the Son of God sounds like pathetic mythology or mild madness to the so-called modern mind. Hollywood at its best can produce a drama of the crucifixion which arouses the sympathetic emotion of a declared agnostic. But who can explain to him that this cruel execution of a good Jew in ancient history has anything to do with the real existence of the agnostic himself—that is, with the forgiveness, however unsought, of the man's sins, however unacknowledged? Further, Easter comes as an annual boon to the needle trade, to dress shops and department stores. Many a good Christian lady celebrates her joy in the resurrection of Jesus Christ by running up her charge account. But how does the Christian who tells of the risen Christ get beyond the shrugging shoulders and the kindly, condescending expression of disbelief in the eyes of his hearer?

Many Christians are properly insistent upon the need to communicate the Gospel in the simple terms of the common man's paltry vocabulary. But this effort at simplification does not easily raise men's understanding above the plane of conventional belief that there must be a 'Divine Being', that the myth of Christmas stimulates kindness and charitable works for a season, and the myth of Easter suggests that the grave may not be the end after all.

This disregard for the true substance of the living apostolic faith is not confined to the extra-ecclesiastical areas where men and women live. Churches themselves have unwittingly assisted in the concealing of the bare elements of the Gospel. It has been easy for an ancient Latin-speaking Church to convince the docile and the credulous that it possesses a rich deposit of divinely dictated doctrinal propositions, but that they as church members need not really believe and think about this deposit. Likewise the members of another large and allegedly methodical Church need not bother about their Twenty-five Articles of Religion, because after all what really counts is having a warm heart and complying with religious and moral duties.

But the first Christians did not devote themselves to theories about a Divine Being nor minimal precepts of cultic observation and moral duty. Nor was the 'faith which was once for all delivered to the saints' (Jude 3) like a dead deposit of gold in Fort Knox, never seen by anyone but its few keepers but theoretically validating the common currency. The Gospel does not belong exclusively to the time of its first reception in Jerusalem, nor among the dust and cobwebs of what the catalogue of Oxonian Blackwell quaintly calls 'Antiquarian Theology'. Though rooted in a definite event at a well-known place at a certain time in history, the apostolic message of Jesus Christ is as living, contemporary and relevant to us now as it was to the apostles then. The apostolicity of the Christian faith is a testimony to the truth of the confession, 'Jesus Christ is the same yesterday and today and for ever' (Heb. 13⁸). This means not only that Jesus Christ is timeless and unchanging in being, but that the work He has accomplished for man's forgiveness and salvation through His ministry, death and resurrection is as applicable now as it was then or ever shall be.

We are brought back to the question repeatedly: How do we devote ourselves to the perennially valid teaching of the apostles, and how do we convey it to men and women today?

Must we become biblical literalists or fundamentalists, jettison the result of a century of critical theology, and hit the sawdust trail? Not at all! Although numerous Christians concur in their rigid convictions about biblical inerrancy and the fundamentalist faith, there is no evidence at all that the saving faith in the crucified and risen Lord is held exclusively by them.

The method of biblical study known as the historical-critical method during the past three generations has come as a timely gift to the Church. Who can show that it has not been a part of God's plan for this era of sky-rocketing intellectual advance and scientific discovery? Unfortunately many good Christians think the word 'criticism' means negation of the Bible's message. On the contrary, textual and historical criticism has liberated the Word of God in the Bible from the restraining chains of obscurantism which over the centuries have bound it. Of course, the biblical critics have at times run to excess and to the detriment of the Christian faith, as in the case of D. F. Strauss and F. C. Baur more than a century ago in Germany, or even to less degree of Rudolf Bultmann today. Nevertheless the critical mode of biblical exegesis is an indispensable means by which to learn that faith does not necessitate the surrender of sanity. This is not to say that a fundamentalist Christian does not have real faith in Jesus Christ. Of course, he does. And he frequently draws others to Christ as well. But the inflexible dogmatism of his biblical interpretation and of his view of the Christian life is so often so cumbersome and unintelligible that it actually alienates many persons who would be drawn to genuine faith in Christ.

If not as fundamentalists, then, how do we know and share the apostolic Gospel? Do we dash to the opposite extreme, blue pencil in hand, to edit out any element of the apostolic tradition which seems to offend common sense or smacks of the supernatural? This is a deceptive snare into which even the very intelligent and sincere Christian can fall. Trying earnestly to find universally persuasive verification of the New Testament claims for Jesus Christ, the events of His life, and the effects of His death and resurrection, such a would-be apologist inadvertently betrays the faith he wants to strengthen. He clutches at shreds of historical and archaeological evidence, hoping to show that if the Bible is factually true in one place it might be more credible in another. He scratches under the tables of biologists and psychologists for such crumbs of their lore as seem to explain Jesus's works of healing or to enhance the possibility of His bodily resuscitation after two nights in the tomb. Or else he scours in a fascinating way the pages of contemporary drama and obscure poetry, rejoicing in their references to sin and redemption, in whatever veiled language or form, and trying to demonstrate thereby that there is some universal truth, after all, in the Christ-image. In appreciation of this labour we may agree that much of this prospecting for theological ore in the non-theological fields is highly important for the faith of the Church. But it seems questionable whether such material can be relied upon to provide empirical evidence and rational clarity for a faith in God's action which is essentially mystery. Faith which requires supporting props ceases to be faith and becomes mere supposition. It is an attitude of the mind resting upon reason rather than a disposition of the whole person derived from both reason and will. It is the Protestant equivalent to the Roman Catholic's acceptance of the miraculous Veil of St Veronica or the Holy Tunic of Trier.

The Gospel is advanced neither by uncritical submission to biblical literalism nor by the findings of strictly secular studies. The intervention of God into the life of man on earth is authenticated by the Bible itself, even after it has been refined in the chemicals of criticism. The Word of God which speaks through the pages of the Bible is verily the *living* Word, even as the Fourth Evangelist declared that the power of life itself was in Jesus Christ, the incarnate Word. The vivifying effect of the Word upon persons and groups which honestly seek to devote themselves to the apostles' teaching as the summation of the biblical message is readily discerned today. In student movements, in areas of missionary growth, in the ecumenical movement, and in congregations where a renewal of authentic faith is being experienced, the intensification of Bible study presents weighty evidence of the astonishing way God uses the Bible for the achieving of His purpose.

Furthermore, in the historical experience of the Church and in the lives of countless Christians who have known the reality of the newness of life in Christ, there is attestation of the saving effect of His ministry, death and resurrection. The irrepressible vitality of the apostolic faith is discerned in the Church's susceptibility to reformation and renewal. It is seen also in the Church's worship through prayer and Sacraments, and in its ability to withstand in the long run every tyranny and intellectual or religious attack.

In this admittedly difficult era for the Church it is discouraging for us Christians to realize that the world for the most part is not really hearing what we say we believe—and, if hearing, not interested in believing. Much of the reason for the Church's frustrating failure to capture men's lives for Christ is precisely the drifting away from the apostolic Gospel. It is the inability of the churches through their preaching, teaching and common life to make it known to the bemused or confused masses of men and women that these churches have as their main purpose the commending of their faith in the one God who has acted decisively in Jesus Christ for the salvation of His creatures.

The word 'apostle' comes from the Greek *apostellein*, meaning 'to send'. In one of its earliest references in Greek usage it had to do with the launching of a fleet to carry an embassy of a government. That meaning still pertains to the apostolic Church. We who are privileged to bear the apostles' message in this generation are like an embassy launched into human history to tell others about the One who has sent us. The quality of our life together in the Church, the openness of the Church to renewal, and the degree of our fidelity to Jesus Christ are all involved in the success or failure of that mission. And these in turn are measured by the teaching and message of the original apostles.

'. . . and fellowship . . .'

THREE

Sharing the New Life

WE LIVE NOW in a time when the members of the 'million-footed manswarm', as Thomas Wolfe loved to call them, are anxious about being more than a 'lonely crowd' and hence are talking a good deal about community. The need for this is obvious, universal and terribly urgent. As communities disintegrate or fail to reproduce themselves, individual persons suffer greater emotional and spiritual difficulties during their relatively brief, often painful and inevitably mortal existence on earth. However sympathetic we may be to man's general need, it cannot be sufficiently emphasized that the genuinely Christian community means nothing in particular if it is thought to be based on human gregariousness in general. This is why the current reappraisal of the biblical teaching concerning Christian life together is highly important. The posters and radio commercials of Pepsi-Cola have had a point in urging mankind to 'Be Sociable!' But it takes living faith in Jesus Christ to transform even persons of warm congeniality into members of the new humanity which he came to inaugurate.

So we read in our basic text that the earliest Christians devoted themselves to the apostles' teaching and fellowship (*koinonia* in Greek). But what real meaning can this apostolic type of community have for the churches of which we are members?

The first thing to be said is that there has never been an explanation of the distinctive quality of the Christians' corporate life except in terms of their apprehension of new life in the new age. This was a part of the *kérygma* as well as of their common experience. They were convinced that the coming of Jesus Christ was the event by which God gave to mankind a new beginning, a new direction and a new hope. Thus had God delivered them 'from the dominion of darkness' and transferred them 'to the kingdom of his beloved Son' (Col 1¹³). Thus they had been 'born anew to a living hope through the resurrection of Jesus Christ from the dead' (1 Peter 1³). And the demonstration of this renascence of the human race was evident in their awareness of the presence and vigour of the Holy Spirit in their lives.

As modern, Western, enlightened Christians we are slightly embarrassed by some of the accounts of the New Testament about the bizarre manifestations and antic behaviour attributed to the Spirit of God. Even as we find it hard to think of the immanent Spirit descending in the ornithomorphic image of a dove, so we are disconcerted by dancing tongues of flame, opening prison doors, and the magic carpet treatment accorded St Philip. But the reality and credibility of Pentecost and its consequences are not dependent upon such startling phenomena. We may even gloss over the *glossalalia*, the ecstatic utterances, without discrediting the New Testament's testimony to the work of the Holy Spirit. For it is clearly seen that His effect was to draw men and women into knowledge and faith in Jesus Christ as Saviour, and to suffuse their lives with the quality of love and righteousness which Jesus mediated to them. This assertion about the Spirit's work is not merely a theory to explain the behaviour of the saints, nor a properly pious manner of attributing man's noble qualities to God. It is excited exclamation and glad testimony on the part of the first Christians concerning the wondrous thing which had happened to them. It was not only the Apostle Paul, but many others like him then and in the generations which have ensued, who could cry out exultantly: 'I have been crucified with Christ; it is no longer I who live, but Christ who lives in me; and the life I now live in the flesh I live by faith in the Son of God' (Gal 2²⁰). This means that fellowship, or *koinonia*, begins with the hearing of the apostles' Gospel, receiving it in faith, and sharing the new life in Christ as a member of the divinely called community.

In the Graeco-Roman civilization of the first century there was nothing in the least unusual about a small religious, cultural or merely fraternal society. Historians have learned that the cities of the Mediterranean coastlands were as replete with clubs, lodges, orders and associations as any town in America today. No doubt the ancients had their equivalents to our membership committees and programme chairmen. The ladies met weekly for earnest study of Seneca or Ovid or other authors chosen by the Scroll of the Month Club, or else to plan benefit rummage sales of slightly-worn togas. And the men of select status reclined at lunch every Tuesday and heard twenty-minute orations on the improved Roman highway system, or the infiltration of godless barbarism as a threat to the Roman way of life. So what was one more new society among the Jews, Greeks, or Roman colonists of Jerusalem, Caesarea or Antioch? The Australian historian, E. A. Judge, writes: 'Whatever the original Jerusalem group may have thought about the character of their society and its government, and whatever affinities it may have had with contemporary Palestinian religious movements, the person who wrote up its affairs a generation later for the information of a Hellenistic public presented it in terms that could not fail to identify it as a religious association of the kind familiar to them.' [1] Presumably the same might have been said about the covenant community of ancient Qum-ran, even though it had a more monastic character than the earliest Church had.[2]

What the contemporary observer could not discern in the early Church was precisely that invisible quality of faith in Christ and the love of Christ which any Christian person may truly possess without always disclosing it. The uncommon property of the Church was literally its commonalty.

To say a fresh, original word about the Christian meaning of

1. *The Social Pattern of Christian Groups in the First Century* (London: Tyndale, 1960), p. 45.

2. An interesting comparison between the Jerusalem church and Qum-ran is found in Sherman E. Johnson's article, 'The Dead Sea Manual of Discipline and the Jerusalem Church of Acts', in *The Scrolls and the New Testament*, edited by Krister Stendahl (N.Y.: Harper, 1957), pp. 129–42.

the Greek *koinonia* is probably not possible any more. Within the past fifteen years there has been a virtual epidemic of desire to define the word and describe its usage in the New Testament. By this time several magazines, associations and co-operative groups have adopted it as a title. Philologists and exegetes have turned over every pebble to learn its meaning in the Acts of the Apostles and Paul's letters.[3] And through all the denominational channels of instruction and discussion have flown interpretative statements about the nature and necessity of *koinonia*. So now it is dismaying to realize that even before the recovering of this concept has had a chance to effect any radical change in the churches, the word has already become so domesticated and popularized as to be a rather wearisome cliché. We all know that the debased idea of superficial fellowship, which many of us had hoped would be either displaced or redeemed by *koinonia*, has apparently prevailed over its would-be corrective. As Sir Thomas Gresham, the sixteenth-century financier, taught us: what is cheap or spurious drives out of circulation the dear and authentic. So, having just about lost hope in the reforming power of true *koinonia*, we are still stuck with the soggy notion of fellowship as it is popularly conceived. We look in vain for an unsullied word to express the kind of divine-human community which is of the essence of the Church. The greatest of seventeenth-century British Independents, John Owen, once referred to it as 'convenient cohabitation', but the subsequent changes in our language have rendered that phrase not only quaint but rather ambiguous. And rejecting the modern jargon, Professor Paul Lehmann has announced that *koinonia* does not mean 'using one another's toothbrush'.

Recognizing that sudden popularity is suffocating this unusually pregnant Greek word, let us recall anyway what the men of the New Testament were trying to communicate by using it.

---

3. The most dependable summary of recent research is found in *Communion with God in the New Testament*, by A. Raymond George (London: Epworth, 1953).

What was the koinonia to which the earliest Church devoted itself?

In an excellent study of the word, J. G. Davies has suggested four distinct biblical meanings.[4] But there is another four-part scheme set forth by the Swiss theologian, Philippe-H. Menoud in his excellent little book, La vie de l'Eglise naissante.[5] He rightly proposes that the full meaning of koinonia comprises four subordinate senses of the word, which he calls: the spiritual, the material, the ecclesiastical, and the eucharistic.

(a) The spiritual meaning is the most familiar: a familiarity which regrettably in recent years has bred contempt, due to distortions of it. In commonplace, pious expression this is the blesséd tie that binds our hearts in Christian love. In its highest form it is the unity of the Holy Spirit in the bond of peace. It is one state of life with a two-fold dimension: both loving God through the mediation of Jesus Christ in the power of the Spirit; and participating in this divine love with one's human brother or neighbour. It is the experience of Christians sharing together in the new life of the Spirit which has been a possibility and a reality since the coming of the Christ.

Some who knew him have said that the late Father Lionel S. Thornton, the influential Anglican theologian, was actually a rather lonely person. Nevertheless he wrote an impressive book on koinonia, the title of which has been widely adopted as a designation of the spiritual reality of this word: The Common Life in the Body of Christ.[6] Thornton's definitive observation is worth pondering: 'As soon as we begin to ask wherein this fellowship consists, it is seen to draw its whole character and significance from its relation to God in and through Christ. . . . The life which we share in common in the Church is not primarily that of a human fellowship. Its distinctive character as manifested in human fellowship is wholly drawn from a divine source, and mediated to us in that fellowship through our joint-participation

4. Members One of Another (London: Mowbray, 1958).
5. Pages 22–3.   6. (London: Dacre, 1942), pp. 47, 327.

in Christ.' Various instances of the use of *koinonia* in the New Testament bear this meaning. Honesty and accuracy with respect to the Bible require us to keep insisting that the source of *koinonia* is the presence and working of God in our human sphere. It is both banal and dishonest to reduce the genius of Christian community to mere congeniality and group activity.

(b) In the sense that it rejects pure spirituality and hallows the common earthy stuff of which we are made, Christianity is properly called a materialistic religion. Having been often reminded of this fact in an age when the word 'materialism' is regarded by many as an obscenity, we should not be astonished that the New Testament presents a *material* sense of *koinonia*. The Jerusalem church may not have had a study programme on problems of economic justice. But it made sure that the economic needs of all the members were supplied by the voluntary and unconditional surrender of property to the common ownership. 'There was not a needy person among them', for the reason that they 'had all things in common' and therefore 'distribution was made to each as any had need' (Acts of the Apostles 2^{44}, 4^{34-5}).

Unlike the Jews ancient and modern, we Western and *bourgeois* Christians may not always find the Cross of Jesus to be a stumbling-block. But we stumble precipitously over the idea that the Gospel might require the sharing of our property. Of course, we can handily explain away this subversive notion if we want to. Historians such as Ernst von Dobschütz have properly assured us that the sharing in the Jerusalem church was entirely voluntary, not mandatory.[7] Ananias and Sapphira found their lives unexpectedly terminated, not because they disobeyed the apostles' orders to pool their capital gains, but for deceiving the Almighty God. And we can explain further that the early Christians were a small and intimate group, that they lived under the fear of an apocalyptic end of history, that St Luke had a marked tendency to idealize this first community, and finally that the pristine

7. *Christian Life in the Primitive Church* (London: Williams & Norgate, 1904), p. 143.

Christian communism must have proved to be unworkable because it is not further stressed in biblical teaching. Truth and falsehood are mixed in such rationalizations.

The power of the early ideal has not been lost in the history of the Church, however. Indeed it has had remarkable persistence. The apologist, Justin Martyr, wrote of the Christians about A.D. 150: 'We who once took most pleasure in the means of increasing our wealth and property now bring what we have into a common fund and share with everyone in need.'[8] Down through the centuries, from the Egyptian desert monasteries to the Hutterite Brethren, the Doukhobors, the Iona Community of Scotland and the Koinonia Farm in Georgia, the practice of full sharing has continued as a witness to the rest of us.

In a modification of this economic koinonia, the General Rules of the Methodist General Societies (which still have a place of prominence in The Doctrines and Discipline, as well as a quaint but disregarded appeal) enjoin Methodists to assist their brethren by 'employing them preferably to others; buying one of another; helping each other in business; and so much the more because the world will love its own and them only'.[9] Whether two neighbouring Methodists who deal in used cars could abide by this rule today is at best dubious. But where the churches have not sold out completely to market-place morality, there are continuing examples of the koinonia in goods. The churches of India are by no means free from the avarice of the natural man. Nevertheless a recent visitor to India reports: 'In the villages, I am told, a Christian is seldom allowed to starve by his fellows. At the synod of the Church of South India a vocal group urged that it was the duty of the Church to find jobs for Christians and to provide the necessary training for them.'[10]

Upon our consciences lies the question of whether we Chris-

8. Apology, I. 14, in Early Christian Fathers, edited by Cyril C. Richardson (London: S.C.M., 1953; Philadelphia: Westminster, 1953), p. 249.
9. 1956 edition, p. 36.
10. John W. Grant, God's People in India (Toronto: Ryerson, 1959), p. 24.

tians, even we who believe that we have not capitulated to the standards of the acquisitive, affluent society in America, can fool ourselves by thinking that occasional charitable hand-outs, subscriptions to the Community Chest, and a dollar a week to the local church are adequate or even minimal expressions of the material *koinonia* which belongs to the nature of the Church.

(c) Related to the material sense of *koinonia* is that which Menoud calls the *ecclesiastical*. What he is talking about is money; but it is not money which represents only a loving concern of the faithful for one another. It is the collection of funds from the churches of Asia Minor and Greece for the aid of the beleaguered Christians of Jerusalem. The collection was stressed several times in the letters of St Paul (Rom 15^{25-8}, 1 Cor 16^{1-4}, 2 Cor 8-9) with such vigour that a Christian today would think that Paul was simply speaking in the manner of a modern fundraiser. But his continual harping on the theme of the collection was not due to his devotion to a balanced budget nor even to his desire that Christian generosity should be nurtured. Many recent biblical commentators have pointed out that Paul was thereby trying to give visible, tangible, and negotiable evidence of the fact that all the churches belonged to one another because of their unity in Jesus Christ; and further, that all the Gentile churches were indebted to the Jerusalem church because of its primacy. As John Knox discerns it, the collection was the major preoccupation of Paul for several years of his missionary activity, because it was 'more than a simple philanthropic act; it had very important ecclesiastical, almost theological, implications. It was a symbol of the unity of the church.' [11] In like manner—but with the exception of deference to any particular church in Jerusalem or Rome or Geneva—the vast programme of Inter-church Aid through the World Council of Churches is today binding churches and Christian groups together through the sharing of medical services, clothing, food and other needs.

11. *The Early Church and the Coming Great Church* (N.Y.: Abingdon, 1955; London: Epworth, 1957), p. 95.

Now a remarkable aspect of this Pauline emphasis upon the collection for the poor saints of Jerusalem is the fact that he twice uses the word *koinonia* in reference to the money itself (Rom 15[26], 2 Cor 9[13]). Note that Paul does not say that the money is a mere representation of the *koinonia*; but this *is* it! How can this name of high spiritual relationship be applied literally to a bag of money? In terms of ancient Greek or modern rational philosophy this would be an absurdity, or at best a piece of poetic licence. But the Hebrew mind feared no absurdity and needed no such licence in such usage. What was the true identity of the money in Paul's collection? It was not a matter of gold or silver metal and the image of Caesar. Its real nature was to be found in its intended use, its potential service. Since the intention of the collection is the strengthening of *koinonia* in the Church, Paul can deliberately declare that the money is the *koinonia*.

Here is an analogy to the question which is so perplexing to the modern mind, even the mind of a well-informed Christian: How can the bread of the Lord's Supper be called in very truth the *body* of Christ? Such language is legitimate and intelligible, not in terms of a mixture of flour and water alone, but of the edible instrument of Christ's presence. 'The true reality of things', writes F. J. Leenhardt, 'is to be found in what God wishes them to be for His creatures.' [12] So the materials which Christians share, whether the cup of cold water or the cup of blessing, whether bread for the hungry or bread from the altar, are the *koinonia* of the Church's life.

(d) This leads us readily to the fourth, the *eucharistic*, use of the biblical word. Of such immeasurable significance for the Church is this meaning that it must await extensive consideration under the 'breaking of bread' in Chapter 6. At this juncture it is enough to cite St Paul's discourse against the worship of idols. Attacking such common and abominable practice, he contrasts

12. *Essays on the Lord's Supper* (with O. Cullmann) (London: Lutterworth, 1958; Richmond: John Knox, 1958), p. 47. Cf. J. G. Davies, *Members One of Another*, p. 29.

with it the deep meaning of eucharistic worship of God in Christ's name. 'The cup of blessing which we bless, is it not a participation (*koinonia*) in the blood of Christ? The bread we break, is it not a participation (*koinonia*) in the body of Christ?' (1 Cor 10[16]). Here in a liturgical action of the congregation, as properly understood and practised, is a conjunction of the several aspects of *koinonia*: the personal fellowship of the faithful ones, their sharing of possessions, their visible unity in Christ, and their spiritual unity with Christ.

It is most improbable that St Luke, as evangelist and chronicler, had in mind all four meanings of the word when he recorded that the earliest Christians devoted themselves to the *koinonia* of the apostles. Yet, the experience of the Church, as seen in the rest of the New Testament, was an unfolding and discovery of the rich diversity of that new concept. This higher dimension of living in the nascent community of the new humanity is conceivable only as a sheer gift of God. Obviously it has been experienced by relatively few congregations of the Church in each passing generation. Apathy, ambition, avarice and apostasy keep hindering the manifestation of that precious *koinonia* which God gives to the Church by His Spirit. Only through their opposites —zeal, humility, generosity and apostolic faith—does this special virtue appear as a historical reality. And then it appears, not in simple restoration of the pattern of the Jerusalem church, but in forms appropriate to varying times, places and peoples.

FOUR

Where Natural Barriers Must Fall

THE CRITERION of apostolic fellowship, with its stark simplicity of Christlike love, looms in awesome judgement over against the distorted and defective community to be seen in numerous churches today. Probably there have been churches in past generations and other places which have been guilty of much greater defection than those of our own time and country. But such comparisons bring us small comfort, and they by no means exempt us from being measured by the apostolic norm. No more irrefutable evidence of our need for reform in this dimension of the Church's life can be seen than in the present tension between the inclusiveness of Jesus Christ and the exclusiveness of many churches.

The abridged Webster dictionary allows the word 'exclusive' to have as one of its meanings 'snobbishly aloof'. Certainly this is the meaning and connotation most appropriate to our society today. It is in this haughty sense that certain clubs, tailors, restaurants and hair-dressers are known as exclusive. And so are certain churches! But could any adjective be more damnably contradictory to the nature of Christ's Church and of any congregation than this?

We are not calling into question the right and even the duty of churches to lay down the terms of membership. It is not rude to exclude persons who do not truly qualify for membership. And the one legitimate basis for membership is the person's sincere faith in Jesus Christ as he is presented in the apostolic witness. Conversely, then, there is but one ground for the exclusion of any persons from the community of the Church, and that is their lack of faith in Jesus Christ or their persistent betrayal of a nominal faith by their words and deeds. Yet even this proper kind of exclusiveness must never be expressed in the manner of snobbish aloofness.

To speak of a church as being an exclusive fellowship for the proper reason just mentioned does not in any sense imply that the church exists only for itself. Neither does it mean that all personal expressions of Christian love are supposed to be confined to the recognized boundaries of the church's membership. In her fine book, *The Witnessing Community*, the French theologian, Suzanne de Dietrich, cites the words of Leviticus 19[33-4]: 'The stranger who sojourns with you shall be to you as the native among you, and you shall love him as yourself; for you were strangers in the land of Egypt.' Thus the Israel of ancient times, she asserts, with all of its external reasons for being an exclusive people, was under God's mandate to impose no restrictions upon hospitality or love towards any person at all.[1] How much less reason for exclusion from its love does the Christian community have, since in Jesus Christ the fullness of God's universal love has been revealed! Yet there are myriad examples of the way churches, or groups of church members, are less disposed to practice the elemental human virtue of friendliness than are many people who have never known of the love of God in Christ. It is not unusual for Christian tourists in the Middle East, for example, to have the experience of finding a warmer, more spontaneously genial reception by Muslims than by Christians. Yet a certain Methodist church in America (and it is by no means unique), which advertises itself as 'The Friendly Church on the Corner—All Welcome', has turned away from its elegant doors a good many Christian brethren—not pagan strangers, but Christians whom God happened to create in His own image but with a dark pigmentation.

We abide by the conviction that the non-discriminating love of God in Christ must be expressed through the members of the Church in such wise that no person is excluded from the effect of that love.

1. (Philadelphia: Westminster, 1958), p. 65.

It is no restriction of love, however, to agree with St Paul that a distinctive demonstration of it is appropriate within the Christian community. 'Let us do good to all men,' advises the apostle, 'and especially to those who are of the household of faith' (Gal 6[10]). Likewise the First Letter of John urges a particular expression of the divine *agape*, or love, on behalf of 'the brethren' who are the church (3[13, 16]). Because of the *koinonia* which Christians have experienced in the Holy Spirit and which they have entered through Baptism, they have a new and uniquely intimate relationship to one another. Their first human allegiance is to other members of the household of God; but this need not, and should not, hinder or weaken their good-will and love towards all persons. These two dimensions of Christian love are rightly distinguished by Kyle Haselden, when he writes: 'It is not to suggest that Christianity is a clannish fellowship in which the special charities of the faith are restricted to the members of the fellowship. But it is to say that between Christian and Christian there should flow lines of communication which do not exist where non-Christians are involved.'[2]

Membership in the Church seems to mean for some people the severing of personal ties and the dropping of loving concern for the outsiders. This is particularly the danger in countries where Christians are a small minority. And in countries like America, where Christians are a majority of all those who have a definite identification with any religion, it is membership in a particular denomination which often occasions such exclusivism. This unfortunate notion is revealed humorously by the sticker on an automobile bumper which warns, 'Drive carefully—you might hit an Episcopalian!' But there is little humour indeed in the various kinds of ecclesiastical isolationism, which imprisons Christians within their own cramped in-group and cuts them off from all persons, Christian or non-Christian alike, who do not belong to it.

Both the narrow exclusiveness and the superficial fellowship of many congregations are due to the commonly held idea that

2. *The Racial Problem in Christian Perspective* (N.Y.: Harper, 1959), p. 188.

Christian community is built upon the mutual congeniality of its selected members. The greater the degree of independence and autonomy of the congregation, the more its members adhere to this belief. Now one ought not to disparage friendliness and congeniality within the household of God. Dismal is the church where they are lacking. But they are an utterly false basis for *koinonia*. The true basis of community is Jesus Christ and faith in him, as attested and sealed by Baptism and expressed through devotion to the Gospel and performance of Christ-like works of love.

There is no valid reason why a congregation should allow itself to fall into, and continue in, the familiar practice of seeking and attracting members who, judged by sociological rather than theological standards, are 'their kind of people'. Birds of a feather may indeed flock together: but the only feather which the Christian flock need have in common is their faith in Jesus Christ. And in a land where all speak the same language, there can be no justification for churches' choosing sides according to such patterns of congeniality as a certain economic class, a certain educational level, a certain social viewpoint, or a certain colour of skin, or any combinations of these.

Whenever Christians permit these natural and secular distinctions to mark out the boundaries of their alleged community, they are in effect denying the reconciling power of the Lord who is the basis of true *koinonia*. Reconciliation and atonement, as taught by the New Testament and held by the Church to be the enduring effect of the life and work of Jesus Christ, either mean that human beings are brought together in a new relationship of forgiveness and love, or else they mean nothing at all. The reality of that divine effect upon men's relationships is not destroyed by the continued exclusiveness of Christians towards one another, but it is concealed and suppressed by it. Of course, the stratification of various congregations according to income brackets, especially in the cities and suburbs, may make it easier to conduct a successful every-member canvass for the annual budget of the church; but it renders impossible the demonstrating of the great truth that rich and poor alike—or even the fairly rich and the very rich—are brothers in Christ. The separating of college graduates in one church and the *illiterati* in another may make sermon preparation easier for the respective pastors; but it defies the fact that the sheep of Christ's flock do not all need an academic sheepskin to belong. It may be regarded as natural, furthermore, that people sharing harmonious views on labour unions, foreign trade tariffs, and a certain political party will be a compatible society; but it is offensively sub-Christian to permit a church to be so constituted. And as for the segregation of white, yellow, red, brown or black Christians in respectively mono-chrome churches, there is towering evidence in the New Testament and in theological reflection that the eyes of faith, once opened wide by the power of Christ, are made colour-blind to all these dermatological distinctions.

Nowhere are the infidelity and impotence of contemporary churches more evident than in their unwillingness and their inability to surmount the barriers of class and race in unredeemed society. The churches of hardly any confession or country are fully innocent in respect to this indictment. Maori Christians in New Zealand and Chinese dispersed through South-east Asia feel the barbs of discrimination by other Christians. In India, despite the notable efforts of church leaders and the government to eradicate caste distinctions, there are still many churches in which membership in a certain caste is more determinative of the course of life than membership in Christ. The churches in America may derive a kind of demonic satisfaction from the knowledge that the segregation of Negroes in South Africa is even worse than in South Carolina or South Chicago, but this scarcely excuses them for the past century of segregation in their own communities and their craven policy of not rocking the boat during the present storm over racial injustices.

The much publicized and undeniable fact that the churches, with relatively few exceptions, are lagging far behind secular organizations in the demonstrating of non-discriminatory brotherhood is an indictment upon them so monstrous that it drives many a sensitive apologist for the Christian faith to an ultimate feeling of grey despair. The current turmoil effecting racial distinctions in human society is marked by both deplorable setbacks and marvellous advances. It is a struggle involving people of all nationalities and religions. The contending for non-segregated society is spurred by a variety of motives, both religious and philosophical. But it is of the utmost urgency for greater numbers of Christians to perceive and believe that the reconciling work of God in Christ, as manifest in the *koinonia* of the Church, leaves absolutely no justification for the exclusion of any faithful Christian from any church on account of his race or national origin. Again to cite the true and incisive words of Haselden: 'The question of whether or not a Negro should be admitted into the fellowship of other Christians should not even be debatable; if he applies as a Christian he does not apply as a Negro. To discuss his admission on the basis of his race is to raise an issue for which there is no room in the Christian conscience or in the Christian community.' [3]

The movement for racial integration in America may be sufficiently swift, as compared to the pace in past decades, to satisfy and encourage many people who desire to see it achieved. Nevertheless, in this brief era of world revolution, when the black and brown majority of the human race no longer pleads for equal recognition but demands it, the pace cannot be too rapid. Nor will it attain its proper pace until Christians, especially those millions in America who are either white or black, see more clearly that the problem of integration is essentially a theological one. In respect to the atoning work of Jesus Christ and the nature of the Church as a unity bound together in love, full integration of people of diverse races is not merely tolerable: it is imperatively needed as an authentic sign of the power of Christ's love among men. Talk about unity and *koinonia* is sheer mockery

3. *The Racial Problem in Christian Perspective*, p. 191.

in any situation or locality where Christians are deprived of participation in the same because of their colour.

Especially in the United States should it be noted that the social acceptability of persons should not be conditioned by their race; for in this land the majority of both the discriminators and the discriminated against are Christians. In the light of this plain statistical fact, it is no exaggeration to assert that the problem of segregation and integration in America is primarily one of the division and unity of the Church.

Appeals to the equality of civil rights which are guaranteed in the United States Constitution certainly have reason behind them and cogency in their application. And such advances as are being made in America in the social and political spheres are to be welcomed, whether they be motivated by democratic political theory or by deep religious convictions. It is hardly justifiable for Christians to minimize the accomplishments of all who do this right thing for different reasons.

But the supreme court of appeal for equality in America is not the Supreme Court of the Federal Government but 'the court of the Lord', the disclosure of God's purpose and His means for achieving it through Jesus Christ and the Church. The message of reconciliation is equally applicable to every form of division within the Church. It is deplorable that the Church is divided between, say, Baptists and Episcopalians. But is it any less a denial of the unity of the Church that white Baptists and Negro Baptists remain segregated in virtually every dimension of life? Since February 1960 the nation has been greatly stirred by the 'sit-in' demonstrations on the part of students and others against traditional barriers to equal rights for Negroes. For the most part this continuing assault upon such barriers has been instigated and sustained by convictions derived from the Gospel. Especially has it been inspired by the vision of a reconciled society brought about through the means of non-violence, suffering and forgiving love. Nothing could be more consonant with the example and teaching of Jesus. And yet, even this noble movement will fall short of its potentialities if Christians by and large fail to see in it a manifestation of both the unity of the Church in the broad sense and the *koinonia* of Christians in each particular place.

It would be foolish for anyone to think that he could persuade others to accept the Christian pattern of an inclusive church, based upon faith alone, by promising that such a congregation would be happier, more solvent financially, or more acceptable to society. Quite the contrary. It is hard enough for genuine Christian fellowship to prevail in a homogeneous church. Even among Christians it often happens that those who scratch each other's backs at one time may stab in the back at another. The more diverse the types of people in a church, the greater the difficulty of mutual understanding and compatibility. And the more the Church might become unlike secular society, due to social and racial integration, the less civic approval it is likely to enjoy. But communal bliss and extensive popularity are goals which no church may legitimately seek for itself. What is the proper and all-important goal towards which the apostolic Gospel and the true *koinonia* of the Spirit point the Church? It is this: the manifestation of the renewed humanity as reconciled and saved by Jesus Christ.

In one sense the church members ought not to be influenced by what other people think: the unpopularity of mixing classes and races should not be a deterrent to a church's living up to its divinely determined character. In another sense, however, they should be exceedingly sensitive to the reaction of outsiders to what is seen in the Church: for the quality of Christian community is a most important concomitant of the Church's mission in all the world.

The world may really begin to believe what Christians are always claiming about the power of God's love and redeeming work in Christ when they see the way in which God can overcome all the grim barriers to human community which now fragment mankind at every level of social existence. There are many doubting, scoffing people who regard the Christian faith as either a superstitious hoax or as a desiccated vestige of a past age of faith. They will not see the evidence of Christ's reconciling power in our day if the churches persist in their craven acquiescence to prevailing patterns of social fragmentation. Not all of them, of course, but many will respond with alacrity and interest when they can behold Christians and the churches taking inevitable risks to manifest the non-discriminatory community which is peculiar and proper to the Church.

We speak blandly, casually, of the 'missionary imperative' of the Church in our time. But an imperative means a command. And if we take this matter seriously, the commander is God Himself. In recognition of the clearly discerned ways in which the exclusiveness of the churches impair this mission to mankind, we are forced to declare that it is imperative for Christians to eradicate any existing barriers to the full membership and fellowship of all in a given place who are Christian. We should be doing this now and in the decade ahead. And we should do it with deliberateness of planning, and with at least the rate of speed of other social revolutions which are at work in the world. This will not come about as a consequence of the merely tepid faith and amicability of the church members. It is God's Spirit working through men which alone can effect such reconciliation and community. But He is obliged to use men and women; and their utility is dependent upon their knowledge of His will, their zeal to have it be done on earth, and their courage and wisdom to work out plans and strategies for Christians to live together in authentic, classless community.

The *koinonia* to which we living Christians can devote ourselves is no less real than that to which the first believers devoted themselves nearly two millennia ago. The quality and essence of it are unchanging. So we are not constrained to look back in longing towards the golden generation, described in Acts 2, when this was a reality in the Church. Having the *koinonia* to a certain degree in this present time, despite all our deficiencies, we may with faith look forward to a still higher experience of its realization.

Our sharing in the new life in Christ will still be characterized by the four-fold pattern of the New Testament *koinonia*. Demands will continue to be made upon us for material sharing, if not quite common ownership. In the unrelenting era of the welfare state and the massive inequities of food and property in mankind's expanding population, we Christians need to plan out and accept new obligations for sharing what we possess through God's grace.

The contemporary form of the ecclesiastical *koinonia* is far more complex than the collection of money which St Paul gathered for the saints of Jerusalem. It involves the immense problem of reducing our separation as denominations or self-sufficient communions. The New Testament certainly knew nothing of denominations in the modern sense of them; and if it had, there is strong reason to think that such ecclesiastical anomalies would have been categorically condemned. For they perpetuate the divisions of the one Church in a manner wholly incompatible with the concept of the Church which the New Testament, and especially Paul, plainly taught. The apostle's collection of money was one device for holding together the Church in its unity. Today we have an astonishing and exciting array of effective devices for the same purpose. Inter-church co-operation in cities and larger regions is an accepted pattern, although its potentialities have by no means been realized as yet because of the tendency of divided churches still to hold back from full participation with each other. Church councils are certainly here to stay, and within them the member churches or denominations are discovering what it means to 'grow together in unity'. (It is worth noting that the World Council of Churches is designated by the Greek Orthodox Church, using modern Greek, the *Koinonia* of Churches.) And throughout the world in country after country the denominations which have lived in mutual estrangement for generations are coming together in church unions, in numbers and at a rate unprecedented in the whole of church history.

The koinonia experienced in the breaking of bread, the Lord's Supper, has yet to be effectively realized by countless Christians. As it will be discussed in Chapter Six, the defective practice of observing this sacrament in some churches is depriving individual Christians of a sense of the depth of the relation they may have with the living Lord as well as with their brethren in the Church. And with respect to the wider effects of the Holy Communion among presently divided churches, we shall see that it exerts a healing power which we have scarcely begun to appreciate.

The spiritual and personal meaning, finally, remains open to us to enjoy. Koinonia is still grounded upon God's gift of our common belief in the apostolic Gospel and faith in Jesus Christ. It still means that through Baptism we participate in the new life of the Holy Spirit; and in very practical, specific ways we can share with our brethren the fruit of the Spirit's working. But this sharing requires a kind of community which our prejudice and social conditions have conspired to restrict in most churches of the present time. And one of the clearest needs before us is our acting upon Christ's love and by his direction to show that, despite any natural or social distinctions of human beings, we who are baptized into Christ are 'one body in Christ, and individually members one of another' (Rom 12^5).

FIVE

All Baptized into One Body

THE FRIGID formality of some churches and the cloying chumminess of others are equidistant from the apostolic experience of the common life in Christ. Neither the cold eye of unrecognition nor the artificially heated handshake belongs to that personal participation in the gifts of God which may rightly be called *koinonia*. And it is a healthy sign that numerous congregations today are earnestly searching for the ways by which this Christian communal life may be effectively expressed in the crowded cities, pleasant suburbs and outlying rural areas of the land.

All of us who desire the renewal of the churches are required to probe the root causes of the present *malaise* in many of them. And if we dig radically enough in search of the defective tissues of faith, we may well find ourselves dealing with Baptism. Probably there are more obvious points of disaffection in the programme of the churches: the commitment of individual members, the substance of preaching, the worldliness of some churches and the otherworldliness of others. Even so, in the prevailing theology and practice of Holy Baptism we are very likely to find the clue to an understanding of what is right or wrong with particular churches. From the very beginning of the Christian Church's existence, Baptism has been the normal manner of entering into the life in Christ. And if *koinonia* is just that life in its fullness, an understanding of the mode of entering it is clearly of great value. Despite the fact that many Christians today have barely the slightest interest in Baptism as such, it cannot be regarded either as extreme sacramentalism nor as biblical obscurantism to maintain that Baptism has this critical import for the real life in Christ of both the individual believer and the whole community.

Just a casual look at the New Testament shows us that the practice of baptizing was indispensable to the normal life of the apostolic church. In the gospels, the Acts of the Apostles, and the epistles it is evident that Baptism belonged to the essential experience of being a Christian. When the first recorded sermon on Pentecost was preached by the Apostle Peter, the Jews who heard and believed were 'cut to the heart' and they asked fervently what they must do. Peter, according to the ancient tradition, simply laid down two requisites: 'Repent, and be baptized every one of you in the name of Jesus Christ for the forgiveness of your sins' (Acts of the Apostles 2[38]). So they were baptized, wrote Luke, and thereupon became the community of those who devoted themselves to the apostles' teaching and fellowship (2[42]). From that hour to the present, both the Church as an institutional community and the individual's experience of renewed life in Jesus Christ have been entered by the same action of water and the Word.

Since we have been maintaining that the genuine Christian fellowship is one which draws its meaning from our common identification with Christ through the working of the Spirit, it is impressive to note how the Church has always felt obliged to seek its style of life according to the historic life of Jesus Christ. This is seen particularly in the practice and meaning of Baptism. Consider the parallel between the story of Jesus in the synoptic gospels and the story of the Church in the Acts of the Apostles. Both accounts have a prominent place for Baptism at the outset: standing in the River Jordan, John the Baptist performs the rite on the One whom he has been anticipating as the Messiah; in Jerusalem the Holy Spirit is poured out as with fire in the Pentecostal Baptism of the Church, whereupon the apostles began that evangelistic summons to repentance and Baptism which has continued ever since. Yet neither in the life of Jesus nor in the history of the Church has the act of Baptism been regarded as merely a ritual action, an empty formality, except by those who have failed to perceive the full significance of Jesus's life as well as the continuing relation of that life to the Church.

The inadequacy of our understanding of Baptism is partly due to the conventional disposition to think of it entirely in terms of the outward appearance and the brief duration of the rite. Ostensibly this is just a Christian variation on a familiar type of religious initiation ceremony; and it can be completed in a matter of seconds. Once done, that's the end of the matter. So it is commonly viewed. Yet, neither in the experience of Jesus nor of the individual Christian neophyte is it to be held that the significance and efficacy of Baptism are contained in the rite of the water and the words alone. If we perceived the New Testament teaching more clearly, we would not allow ourselves to tread such thin theological ice as we do whenever we try to explain Baptism exclusively in terms of the familiar ritual.

Implicit in various passages of the New Testament is the common belief that Baptism has to do with the whole self-giving life of Jesus and with the Christian's whole experience of being one with him in the life of faith. Numerous essays on Baptism have pointed this out. On this interpretation both Karl Barth and his Basel colleague Oscar Cullmann agree, although they disagree sharply on infant Baptism.[1] The Baptism of Jesus makes sense only when it is extended from the River Jordan to Gethsemane and Calvary. It was not just a symbolic washing of himself, but was acceptance of the role of the Suffering Servant with its inevitable culmination in death.

It is the evangelist Matthew who expresses the perplexity of the Christians' thought on Jesus's willing submission to the rite of Baptism for the remission of sins (3^{13-17}). Was it possible for Jesus to confess sins and seek forgiveness as did any other man?

1. Their two small books constitute a most stimulating debate on this subject: Karl Barth, *The Teaching of the Church regarding Baptism* (London: S.C.M., 1948); and Oscar Cullmann, *Baptism in the New Testament* (London: S.C.M., 1950; Chicago: Regnery, 1951).

'John would have prevented him' and rather submit to Jesus's hand. But Jesus replied: 'Let it be so now; for thus it is fitting for us to fulfil all righteousness.' Commentators and theologians are now inclined, with good reason, to interpret this rather enigmatic saying of Jesus in the light of His conscious undertaking of the work of the Servant of God. In Isaiah 53[11] it is the Servant as the 'righteous one' who will 'make many to be accounted righteous'. The words come readily to mind in connection with Jesus's response to the reverent protest of John the Baptist. So Jesus vicariously enters into the sin of 'the many', exhibiting an incarnate solidarity with mankind which is the presupposition of his work as the One who atones and saves.

This inherent connection between Baptism and the life of Jesus Christ is revealed again in Mark's account of the request of James and John for positions of prestige. To this supreme example of the disciples' *gaucherie*, coming immediately after Jesus's prediction of His passion in Jerusalem, the response of their Teacher must have come as a jolt to their consciences. Could they also drink His cup of suffering? Could they be baptized with the Baptism with which He would soon be baptized—a veritable Baptism in blood on the Cross? Yes, they were able, they said. Such would be their suffering, Jesus promised (Mk 10[38-40]). This meaning of Baptism for the whole life and ministry of Jesus is summarized succinctly by George Every: 'Our Lord's baptism is His whole ordeal, from the Jordan, through the temptations, to Jerusalem, death and resurrection.'[2]

St Paul was even more articulate and insistent with regard to interpreting Baptism in respect to the vicarious suffering of Jesus. (It is true that Paul said he refrained from practising Baptism in Corinth, lest it be thought that persons were baptized in his own name rather than that of Jesus Christ. So Corinthians 1[14-17]. But elsewhere in his writing Paul is most eloquent about the deep meaning of Baptism.) Baptism means nothing less than a personal identification of the believer with Christ in the death

2. *The Baptismal Sacrifice* (London: S.C.M., 1959), p. 28.

and burial of the Lord (Rom 6⁴, Col 2¹²). To be baptized really means to know that one is so joined by faith to Christ that he participates in the painful self-giving of the Lord: he has a share (the Greek is *koinonia*!) in the sufferings of Christ (Phil 3¹⁰). Nor is this intended by Paul to mean an experience which is merely individualistic or mystical. Such language about Baptism is in the same category as Paul's very frequent references to a believer's being 'in Christ'. It means life in the new community, the Church, for which Christ readily gave Himself. Baptism introduces the person to partnership, or *koinonia*, in the corporate congregation of the faithful (Phil 1⁵). Likewise it means that the member of the Church enjoys communion, or *koinonia*, in the Holy Spirit (2 Cor 13¹⁴). Being baptized, in short, whether as an infant upon the Church's anticipation of that person's faith, or as a believer on profession of faith, means the outward, sensible, dramatic expression of that movement whereby the person is led by God into the new life in Christ.

Now let us shift attention from the biblical teaching to the present life of the Church. We are well aware of the difficulties which confront us when we try to interpret the conventional rites of Baptism in accord with such sense of personal identification and participation with Christ as the New Testament teaches. But this much ought to be obvious: even as the Baptism of Jesus was not limited in time to that moment or so when He went with John into the Jordan, so in the case of Christians the effect of Baptism is not confined to the time and action of the rite itself. Baptism means being brought into a continuing life, becoming part of an onward process of salvation, during which one is ever threatened and dragged backward by sin, and yet in which one who retains his faith is sustained by the grace of God. Can that be believed today by the millions of men and women who have been baptized in the name of the Triune God?

In a society which 'christens' atomic submarines with a magnum of champagne and 'christens' babies with drops of water sprinkled from a rose, the task seems almost hopeless. But if intensive theological teaching and effective instructional preaching will not bring about a change in thinking about Baptism and the Christian life, the force of political circumstances one day may do so. Already this has happened in East Germany, or the *Deutsche Demokratische Republik*. As is rather well known, but not sufficiently well understood in the West, the Communist government of the DDR has been trying for fifteen years literally to stamp out Christianity. They have decided that even the formalized *Kultur*-conditioned Lutheran churches constitute too dangerous an opposition to the complete triumph of communism. And despite the magnificent resistance and the deepening faith of numerous Christians who have not sought to escape their homeland—and despite the popular myth that a church made up of martyrs cannot really be lost—it is becoming increasingly doubtful whether the Christians of East Germany can resist and exist indefinitely.

One of the strongest leaders of the Evangelical churches of the DDR is Günter Jacob, who is also a valuable participant in the work of the World Council of Churches. Recently he reported how the struggle against the tyrannical government has now come to a focus on Baptism.[3] Previously the communists had decreed that all young people would have to participate in a political parody of the rite of confirmation, called the *Jugendweihe*, or Youth Dedication. In this ritual the State is simply made the substitute for God, and the communist society for the Church. But now the government has moved its knife closer to the jugular vein of the Church by instituting a mandatory offering up of children in a pagan name-giving ceremony. This is a grotesque travesty on Baptism. It places parents in the critical position of having to decide to acquiesce, and thus be guilty of an apostasy from the faith, or to resist and suffer the economic, political, and perhaps corporal punishment. It is no wonder that so many have fled the country by night, risking death at the

3. *Minutes of the Faith and Order Commission, St Andrews, 1960* (Geneva: World Council of Churches, 1960), pp. 49–56.

border of West Germany rather than remain under this duress. But what of the Christians who perhaps rightly have chosen to remain?

Once again in a vestigial area of Western Christendom it has become dangerous to be baptized! This has frequently been the case for Christians in the realms of Islam. In Hindu and Buddhist cultures it was still taken for granted that Baptism means the inevitable sundering of family ties and possibly the risk of discriminatory jeopardy in society. But now it is in Europe that the danger returns, where only two generations ago the pattern of baptizing all non-Semitic babies was just as routine, conventional and non-theological as it has become in large segments of American society. As Dr Jacob declared, the communist threat is 'only knocking down façades which were already crumbling', since Baptism has been a 'hollow tradition' which is disastrous for both the individual and the Church.

So the leaders of the East German churches have acted by laying down stringent disciplines. The faith of parents must be convincingly attested before their children may be baptized. Courses of study in the meaning of Baptism have been intensified. The responsibility of the whole congregation for the faith of fellow members and their children is now emphasized. The baptismal ceremony, once held in the living-room within the context of a family party, is now celebrated during the morning worship of the congregation. In view of these precautions, the legitimacy of both infant's and believer's Baptism and of various forms of administration is recognized as not jeopardizing the true meaning of this initiatory induction into the new life in Christ.

The lesson to be learned by churches in other lands from the harrowing experience of the brethren in East Germany is obvious. In some form or other a political or social crisis might come to countries where the churches now enjoy freedom to do as they please. Before such a crisis comes, or before the façade crumbles and, in falling, discloses our hollowness, we have opportunity to recover a sense of seriousness for the authenticity of every Christian's faith in accord with the apostolic Gospel, as well as to recapture the reality of sharing in the life of Jesus Christ. This involves our sharing in His suffering and love and risen power, and hence in the common life of the Church. Of this quality of Christocentric faith and shared life Baptism is the sign and seal.

It is not only in East Germany that a crisis exists in respect to the practice of Baptism and the implications of it for the well-being of the churches. The crisis touches virtually every church in every land. And a recognition of it should impel Christians to accept a far more faithful responsibility than is now the case. To be more specific, there is a duty of pastoral care laid upon every member of the Church, and most emphatically upon the ordained minister. Just as Christ the Good Shepherd came to seek and to save the lost, so do baptized Christians enlist in carrying on His ministry of salvation. This means that each must have a serious concern for the authenticity and integrity of the faith of both himself and his brother in the Church, as well as a sense of responsibility about those who are not members of the Church but are likely to become such.

Let us consider, first, how a deepened understanding of Baptism might impel us to act towards those who are either uncommitted to the Gospel while inclined towards faith, or else included nominally in the Church but negligent of the Gospel.

(a) In the mission to non-Christians the churches must face the question of their conviction concerning the indispensability of Baptism for admission to the life in Christ. Especially in the various cultures of Africa and Asia, which are dominantly non-Christian in tradition and character, it is being asked whether converts to Christ should incur the painful rejection by family and society which is often consequent upon their being baptized. As in the time of persecutions in the early centuries of the Church, so again today there are growing numbers of persons who are secretly baptized, lest they suffer kinds of reprisal in the communities where they live. Still others make covert profession of faith in Christ and attend worship in churches, but will not take the step of being baptized, for fear of the social and economic ostracism they will suffer. Such instances are most frequently found in lands of Islam, but also in Hindu India. What counsel should they be given by church members? It is easy enough to say that Baptism is just a formality, that salvation does not depend upon it, that one can be a good Christian without it. But does the New Testament, or the example of the apostolic church, give us any warrant for such a facile circumvention of the problem? Surely it does not. There is no firm ground in faith for prudentially avoiding suffering for the cause of Christ, since in the long run the vitality of the person's faith, or of a church's fidelity, may depend upon the person's willingness to suffer. Moreover, it should not be overlooked that Baptism as a public act in a pagan culture can be a powerful means of evangelical witness.

(b) In countries which are traditionally Christian, however they may fail really to qualify for that name today, the churches which practice Infant Baptism must become bolder and more rigorous in making decisions concerning the acceptance and rejection of little children for Baptism. Without here entering that theological wrestling-ring where the struggle over the legitimacy of Infant Baptism goes on, we can still call for a greater firmness. If it is not evident that the parents are faithful Christians and the home environment more than minimally Christian, should the child be baptized simply upon the request of the parents? Social convention is often a stronger motive for making this request than is Christian conviction. Would a pastor's refusal to baptize the child because of the parents' dubious state of faith result in even further alienating the parents from the Church and reducing the chances of the child's ever being baptized? Or would the parents, confronted afresh with the promises as well as the clear obligations of church membership, be more disposed to prepare themselves for sponsoring the Baptism of the child? One can never be sure of the consequences of a gentle rebuff. But the risk is worth taking, lest the grace of God, membership in the Church, and faith in Christ be made to seem even cheaper than they now appear to be.

(c) And what about those baptized members of the Church who are clearly inclined to fall away from the faith? Obviously the rite of Baptism cannot guarantee sustained faithfulness and persistence in the Christian life. Since numerous Christians neglect the grace of God and resist the Holy Spirit by ignoring or violating their baptismal vows, the churches are constrained to exercise a wise, merciful but supple discipline. Churches today can afford neither arrogance nor carelessness in their pastoral care for the nominal members. Their purpose is always to call back the negligent and support the weak. The difficulties of administering a discipline which displays both the tenderness and the virility of Jesus Christ are manifest, but they are not a valid excuse for avoiding it. And when any baptized persons consciously and deliberately reject the requirements of the Gospel for their faith and life, the churches ought not to shrink from the implications of this apostasy. Excommunication is a weapon which can be horribly misused, as it has been exhibited in history. But soft-heartedness in the face of exercising it is no virtue if in fact it expresses a soft and invertebrate faith. Baptism is not undone and eradicated by apostasy, but remains as a sign of judgement upon the person. 'The seal which identifies the soldier of Christ then serves, as Augustine said, to "convict the deserter".'[4]

Other questions of a pastoral nature are raised, secondly, with respect to the Baptism and status of Christians who sincerely try to live responsibly in the Church. Individual churches and denominations ought to be willing to indulge in some honest self-criticism, and accept the criticism of others, in reference to their practice and estimation of Baptism.

(a) No eyebrow is arched when someone declares that conflict-

4. *One Lord, One Baptism*; Commission on Faith and Order (London: S.C.M., 1960; Minneapolis: Augsburg, 1960), p. 67.

ing understandings of Baptism and differing modes of administration of it are included within the whole of Christianty. Most Christians assume a live-and-let-live attitude towards Baptists, Paedo-Baptists, Immersionists, Catholic Sacramentalists, and Quakers. The line between tolerance and indifference is not easy to discern in such an attitude. There are real issues of the truth of the Gospel at stake in the discussion of these varying and opposing conceptions of Baptism. These will not be settled by polemics, anathemas and ridicule on the one hand, nor by unconcerned disinterest on the other. They require study and dialogue among the opposing parties in a frame of mind which is sober, patient and well informed. And since about 1955 there have been many such discussions of Baptism among churches related to the Ecumenical Movement, the results of which are already proving to be more salutary for Christian unity than any could have predicted.[5]

Certainly the least which leaders of churches can do in this regard is to expose prejudices, clear up confusion of thought, and avoid the undue excitement, injury or inhibition of consciences. Because there is but one Lord of the one Church, there is but one Baptism, however variously it may be understood and practised. But careful attention should be directed towards the distinction between ritualistic regularity in the Church and the efficacy of God's grace. The singularity of Baptism and the reality of grace are not jeopardized, much less annulled, by the variety of usages of words and water.

(b) The frequent transfer of members of one denomination or confession to another often raises the question of recognition of baptized persons as true Christians. This is most acute, of course, where churches are involved which are disposed to call false the baptismal practices of other churches. Yet, a reading of the

5. For example, the agreements reached by Lutheran and Reformed theologians in Europe; studies in the Commission on Faith and Order of the World Council of Churches; the church union plans in North India/Pakistan and Ceylon which would unite Baptist churches with those practising Infant Baptism. For an excellent summary, see the special issue of *Encounter* (of Indianapolis), XXI. No. 3 (1960).

history of Christian liturgy reveals a fact worth pondering: namely, that the baptismal practices of all churches today are probably more different from the practice of the early Church than they are from one another. And since it is generally agreed that God, not man, is the primary actor in Baptism, leading His children into the new life in Christ, the refusal to recognize the action of God in the Baptisms within other churches should be viewed with the sharpest disdain. Likewise there should be sufficient recognition of the biblical and theological doctrine that Baptism is once-for-all and unrepeatable so that some churches could be dissuaded from their insistence upon baptizing new members in a second and different manner.

(c) Churches which hold to the baptizing of believers upon profession of faith, and these only, have developed in some places the practice of 'dedicating' infants to the service of the Lord. Within such churches this is considered right and meaningful. Yet, the act of dedication ought not to be equated with infant Baptism, as many erroneously regard it. This both offends the conscience of Christians who stoutly hold to believer's Baptism, and it confuses the understanding and dilutes the doctrine of those in churches which baptize infants.

(d) We have seen above that an essential meaning of Baptism is its leading the person into the common life of the congregation. But a serious obstruction to the clear impact of this meaning upon the mind of the candidate or of his sponsors—and indeed of the congregation as a whole—is the persistence of the practice of private Baptism. Whether in the person's home or the intimacy of a small prayer chapel or other room of a church, it is an impairment of the significance of Baptism. The character of the Church as the Body of Christ, as a koinonia of members, requires the act of baptizing to be done normally in the presence of the whole congregation with the prayerful participation of all.

(e) Churches are constantly tempted to accept indiscriminately as many persons as show willingness to join them through Baptism. This temptation is no less dangerous to churches which baptize believers only than to those which accept infants. Especially in areas where certain churches are established de jure, as are the Lutherans in Sweden, or simply de facto, as are the Baptists in, say, Oklahoma, this temptation is almost irresistible. And a kindred threat to a church's integrity is at work wherever there is an inordinate compulsion to increase the number of converts or new members in order to give public evidence of statistical growth. Unless care be taken to ascertain the true ground of faith for the willingness to be baptized, whether in the mind of the alleged believer or in the parents or sponsors of the infant, a policy of easy acceptance may be pursued which really works to the detriment of the Church.[6]

(f) A minimized theology of Baptism may be due to a partial blindness of some Christians to the objective, saving work of God in Jesus Christ which the apostolic witness sets forth as the basic faith of the Church. It is encouraging and instructive to note that precisely those local churches and denominations which have been making earnest effort to provide satisfying education in the faith and training in faithful discipleship have come to a new level of appreciation for Baptism. When they see Baptism not as a perfunctory ritual of initiation into this religious society but as the establishment of a relation of faith in Christ which is bound up with the whole of a person's life in both time and experience—when churches see this, their programmes of nurture and education in faith and discipleship are given a particular force and instancy. The radically ethical content of the Christian faith, for example, with its requirement of vicarious love and self-giving, is enhanced by the baptismal insight into the dying and rising of the Christian with Jesus Christ. The teaching on the atoning effect of Jesus's life and death, the grace

6. I acknowledge that exception may be taken to this judgement in the case of the mass conversions of tribes in primitive societies. This point, however debateable, is capably pressed by Donald A. McGavran, How Churches Grow (N.Y.: Friendship Press, 1959).

of God, and the present power of the Holy Spirit is likewise given force and focus by the better understanding of Baptism.

(g) Finally the oneness of Baptism as an expression of the reconciling, unifying work of Jesus Christ challenges the churches to re-examine not only their diverse view of Baptism but, much more, their actual reasons for permitting the perpetuation of church divisions. It would be foolhardy, though true in a limited way, to assert that the concept of the one Baptism constitutes a simple solution to the very complex problems of division. Nevertheless it is a potent means for testing the integrity of the matters of faith and practice which presently divide the churches. Baptism testifies to the faithfulness and love of God for the salvation of us creatures through our identification with the one Christ. Baptism presupposes the possible existence of only one Church, and of the common life of Christians under the one Spirit. The one Baptism precedes the one Eucharist, or Lord's Supper; and the wide recognition of valid Baptism across the lines of divided churches calls into sharp judgement the practice of those same churches excluding one another's members from the Table of the Lord. Baptism is, finally, an indispensable element in the reconciling mission of God to all nations and all generations, and thus it judges all temporal and transient obstacles to the manifesting of the Church's unity in the fulfilling of its mission.

'. . . to the breaking of bread . . .'

SIX

Overcoming Lethargy in Liturgy

TO WHAT EXTENT do the diverse churches throughout the world today continue in their liturgical practice the essential elements of worship in the apostolic church? If the criterion of apostolicity applies to the confessed faith and the corporate life of the churches, does it refer equally to the liturgy?

It has been maintained earlier that a deliberate repristination of the form and the manner of life of the New Testament community is neither needful nor possible. History has meaning for the Church because it is the temporal sphere in which the Holy Spirit is working. God did not establish in the first Christian generation a pattern of organization and common life which was immutable for all ensuing generations. According to time, geography and circumstance there have been many legitimate modifications of the form of the Church. Nevertheless there remains a basic quality or character which is preserved in the faith and the life of the Church, however God may have caused or permitted other changes to take place. So also in respect to worship, within the stream of history an impressive and at times bewildering variety of liturgical patterns has been developing without necessarily impairing the basic meaning of worship as held in the apostolic church.

As one travels about the world today, visiting numerous churches along with the other sights which attract tourists, he cannot avoid being amazed at the diverse array of liturgical customs and forms: the Roman Mass in Latin; the several Eastern rites, notably the Divine Liturgy of St John Chrysostom; the Holy Qurbana of the Syrians; the Anglican Order used in many lands with only slight variations; the Lutheran High Mass in Sweden; the stark and restrained rituals of some Protestant churches and the casual, informal services of others. Is any one of these especially close to the apostolic order? Can one of them more than others rightly claim to be an undeviating reproduction of the New Testament pattern?

The continuing conflict of the positive claims or unavowed presuppositions of the many churches tends to drive one towards sheer relativism. With varying intensity of conviction, each asserts its continuity and consistency with the New Testament way of worship, even while admitting that the biblical pattern is far from being explicit and orderly.

It is to be expected that Christians are disposed to see in their own distinctive traditions a true reflection of the apostolic criterion. Bishop Stephen C. Neill once observed that whenever Karl Barth thinks and speaks of the Church, he has in mind an ancient edifice in a small village of the Bernese Oberland, with a tall belfy, a prominent pulpit—and Karl Barth preaching in the pulpit. So Christians generally read about the breaking of bread in the Acts of the Apostles 2[42] and 1 Corinthians 11 and conclude rather quickly that the early churches gathered to worship and celebrate the holy supper in the same mode as their own.

During a visit to the Syrian Orthodox churches of India I was told by their Catholicos (a saintly, bearded man who might have stepped off an El Greco canvas) that the solution to the problem of church divisions was really quite simple. Each church must just begin celebrating the Holy Communion according to the ancient Liturgy of St James, inasmuch as all wise and informed Christians know that James himself received the instructions for this ritual from his brother, Jesus. So who could dispute its authority? A Western Protestant may smile in condescension at this naïve belief. And yet it is probably less untrue to history than the barren notion held by some Protestants that the breaking of bread in the church of the New Testament was nothing more than a common meal such as any Jewish group would enjoy, with appropriate prayers of thanks to God. Such Christians are further inclined to judge that all eucharistic practice in the church life of nearly two thousand years is simply the accumulation of arbitrary innovations and man-made traditions.

The numerous studies of early liturgy, which have appeared in recent years, give little comfort to the advocates of either extreme interpretation. The champions of the idea that the early Church knew nothing more than a simple fellowship meal—like an ordinary church supper today—can point to the bare description in the Acts of the Apostles 2[42, 46]. The Christians continued in attendance at the Jewish temple to offer prayers, and then gathered at one another's home for the breaking of bread. What was unusual about this? Did not pious Jews of the time always begin a meal by giving thanks to God and breaking bread? Even the drinking of wine from a common cup was by no means a Christian innovation. And there were at least two types of Jewish table celebration which might have been the prototype of the Last Supper of Jesus and the Lord's Supper of the Christians. A scholarly debate, which is interesting but inconclusive, has been dealing with the question of whether the Jewish kiddush (a religious meal for men only) or the chabûrah (celebration by a confraternity) lay behind the Christians' breaking of bread—or whether these had no influence upon Christian worship at all.[1] But we know certainly that the disciples frequently ate their meals with Jesus, that they remembered a uniquely significant supper with Him on the night He was betrayed, and that they witnessed to a meal with the risen Lord at Emmaus and perhaps elsewhere. The connection between the breaking of bread in the apostolic community and these meals with the Lord seems beyond dispute. But in what way was the simple rite of breaking bread also related to the developing eucharistic practice of the Church?

1. The reader is referred to W. D. Maxwell's support of the kiddush, in An Outline of Christian Worship (London: Oxford, 1949), pp. 5ff; to Dom Gregory Dix's theory of chabûrah in The Shape of the Liturgy (London: A. & C. Black, 1945), pp. 50ff; and doubts cast on both theories by J. H. Srawley, The Early History of the Liturgy (Cambridge: University, 2nd edn, 1957), p. 3, and J. Jeremias, The Eucharistic Words of Jesus (N.Y.: Macmillan, 1955; Oxford: Blackwell, 1955), p. 26.

According to a well-known thesis of the eminent German scholar, Hans Lietzmann (who died in 1942), the simple meal of fellowship was indeed the practice of the Jerusalem church as described in the Acts of the Apostles 2. But it was the Apostle Paul, he contended, who was the originator of the liturgical meal which was consciously and exclusively identified with the Last Supper of Jesus with the wondering disciples in the Upper Room. It was the liturgical service of Paul as practised by the Greek-speaking Christians rather than the unadorned meal of the Jerusalem community which ultimately prevailed in the Church. It is the Pauline form, then, which has gathered into it the rich assortment of meanings arising from the suffering and death of Jesus, His being raised from the dead, and the profound experience of Christians as being members of His community, the Body of Christ. Thus Hans Lietzmann discerned two quite distinct and irreconcilable practices: the simple one continued for a time in Jerusalem and Egypt, but died out by attrition; the eucharistic liturgy gained momentum and spiritual power as the very centre of Christian worship.[2]

That there were diversities of liturgical practice during the first fifty years after Pentecost is beyond dispute. But the historical evidence turned up by scholars indicates that Lietzmann, while rightly distinguishing the Pauline and Jerusalem types, was not quite justified in calling them irreconcilable. There seems to be a higher degree of accuracy in the conclusion drawn by the late Swedish archbishop, Yngve T. Brilioth. He held that the early Church could hold together both the concept of the common fellowship meal as well as a remembrance of the disciples' last meal with their Lord. After all, Jesus Himself had combined in the Last Supper both the common Jewish type of religious meal and the special symbolical action whereby He interpreted His

2. *Mass and Lord's Supper* (Leiden: Brill, 1953), pp. 205–6, and also *An die Korinther I–II* (*Handbuch zum Neuen Testament,* 9) (Tübingen: Mohr, 1949), p. 58.

impending death in terms of the bread and the cup.[3] And especially in Protestant churches today these two concepts of the Lord's Supper are maintained.

When a comparison is drawn between the congregation of New Testament times and the congregations of which most Christians today are members, there is a sharp contrast to be noted with respect to the diligence of participating in the holy meal. Such a comparison is permissible if it is proper to consider the breaking of bread in the Acts of the Apostles 2 and elsewhere as referring to the original form of the Holy Communion; and there is ample reason so to regard it. The Greek words used to describe the apostolic practice are vivid and forceful. The Christians 'devoted themselves to', or they 'persisted obstinately in' the breaking of bread, in a mood of 'exultant joy' and with a 'transparent sincerity'. This they did 'day by day' in un-diminished, joyous diligence. The trumpet blasts and exuberant musical shouts of J. S. Bach's Mass in B-minor are an expression of the attitude of the earliest Christian worshippers.

If the normative style of eucharistic worship be found in this apostolic community, which was devoted daily to the breaking of bread, we are obliged today to ask ourselves whether we also devote ourselves. (By this word is not meant the popular act of 'devotion' to the material of the Blessed Sacrament, which is widespread among the faithful of Roman Catholicism. Rather is implied the regular participation in the corporate act of Holy Communion with the requisite faith and understanding which make it of supreme religious significance.) With what degree of faith, joy, and vigour of mind and spirit do we and our fellow members now keep this feast of the Lord? Let each answer candidly.

There is a growing conviction among thoughtful Protestants, particularly in America, that so many churches have drifted away from a normative observance of the Lord's Supper that a situa-

3. *Eucharistic Faith and Practice, Evangelical and Catholic* (London: S.P.C.K., 1930), p. 12.

tion of stark crisis exists. It was not a 'high church' liturgiologist but the Congregational New Testament scholar, C. H. Dodd, who wrote of the Lord's Supper: 'In this Sacrament the whole of what our religion means is expressed.'[4] He did not exaggerate. Both the lukewarm, poorly informed Christian and the casually observing outsider may see little more in this sacred rite than a religious ceremony with some inspirational values which can be explained psychologically. But the countless Christians who have sustained their participation in the Lord's Supper can witness to the truth of Dodd's assertion. Especially if they have learned of the biblical, historical and theological background of the familiar ritual action and words, they are able to testify that in their experience the fullness of life has been opened to them by faithfully accepting this gift of God. And yet, the number of those in the churches who are virtually oblivious to such an appreciation of the sacrament is alarmingly great.

The churches include thousands of members who are of the same mind as the visitors to the National Gallery of Art in Washington, D.C., when they gaze in astonishment at a certain picture. It is a depiction of the Holy Communion by the talented but often weird artist, Salvador Dali. At first glance it reminds one of the universally admired illustration of the Last Supper by Leonardo da Vinci. But on closer inspection one perceives the marks which make this painting unique. The host at the table is not the Lord Jesus soon to be put to death; it is the risen Lord who has become, in the artist's idea, wholly detached from earth, matter and space. Jesus's body is diaphanous, suggesting a mode of existence which is of neither earth nor heaven. The details, such as the disciples' heads and the cup of wine, are drawn with a skill almost shocking in its brilliance. No doubt thousands of viewers have derived both aesthetic satisfaction and some religious meaning from the large painting. But all things considered, it is only honest to conclude that Dali has revealed a misconception of the Holy Communion which is deep and wide-

4. In *Christian Worship*, edited by N. Micklem (London: O.U.P., 1936), p. 82.

spread. People see the picture exactly as they see the sacrament: impressive, beautiful, obviously religious—but expressing neither reality nor mystery.

Knowing little of the divine reality and mystery which are inherent in the Communion, many Christians have decided to celebrate it very seldom in their churches and even then to attend with diffidence. It is hard to prove which of these two negative factors comes first, the lack of perception or the infrequency of participation. Dullness of understanding and carelessness about attendance seem to reinforce each other to the detriment of the life of both the individual and the church. Adequate perception and frequency, on the other hand, work together for the upbuilding and strengthening of the Christian life.

Two issues are thus involved in the present crisis of Communion: first, diligence and frequency of participating in it; and second, comprehension of what is believed to happen in it.

How often should there be a celebration? Is there a norm of frequency? In some Protestant churches it is a monthly service, in others only quarterly. In the latter case, if a person should have to miss a Communion service because of some domestic indisposition, he has to go several months without experiencing that act to which the apostolic community devoted themselves and which has been a main source of inspiration and nourishment for the best of Christians through all generations. In more than a few churches, moreover, the members are so poorly instructed in the meaning of the sacrament, or they have been so bored by certain ways of observing it, that they actually look upon the Communion Sunday as a time when they feel justified in staying at home! This situation is too familiar to require further description. It is no wonder that many serious Christians, and not only the pastors and theologians, ponder in pessimism how something can be restored to the churches which is almost wholly lost and not even missed.

In this day, when the world-wide movement for church unity and mission has caused a reaction of denominational defensiveness, it is increasingly popular to support one's views with proof-texts from the writings of the denomination's founder. This is nothing new to Lutherans, who have traditionally been able to close any argument by citing a relevant sentence of the blesséd Dr Martin Luther. With only a bit less vigour, Presbyterians have found their authority in the solemn writings of John Calvin. And now the American Methodists are following the British mode of finding appropriate tests from John Wesley or the hymns of his brother Charles. This is certainly a legitimate procedure if we intend to be faithful adherents to our denominations, even while seeing them in relation to the wholeness of the universal Church. And if we accept the authority of these founders, it is important to emphasize that Luther, Calvin and Wesley all urged their followers to share in the *Abendmahl* or *Sainte-Cène* or Lord's Supper at least once every week.

The practice of John Wesley is particularly impressive. As Gordon Rupp, the British historian, has written of him: 'He found peculiar force in the fact that this sacrament was instituted by "the plain command of Christ", and asserted that since "we are bound to obey every command of God as often as we can . . . it is the duty of every Christian to receive the Lord's Supper as often as he can".'[5]

Some have argued against weekly celebrations on two grounds. First, that familiarity breeds contempt; the holiness of the service tends to be minimized or impaired by too frequent observance. Second, that sacramental worship easily becomes a convenient escape from carrying out the practical work of the church from day to day.

The first argument is refuted by the experience and faith of countless devoted Christians who as a matter of regular habit share in the weekly Communion. It is well known that many Episcopalians are committed to such regular practice. Likewise the members of the Christian Churches (Disciples of Christ)

5. In *The Holy Communion*, edited by Hugh Martin (London: S.C.M., 1947), p. 114.

make weekly Communion an integral part of their worship. Can it be shown that these Christians therefore hold a view of the sacrament which is less reverent and discerning than that of Christians who communicate monthly, quarterly, or just annually? One would hesitate, moreover, to assert that the daily celebration of the Mass, required of each Roman Catholic priest, makes him treat it as a perfunctory ritual. If frequency does breed contempt, could we not on that argument put morning worship and preaching itself on a monthly or quarterly schedule?

But is the sacrament an escape? Do pastors and members who find the world too much for them and the work of the Church too difficult let themselves be deceived into thinking that celebrating and communicating at the table are all they have to do? The temptation to let this be an escape from responsibility is a real but by no means inevitable one. In the almost moribund church life of highly secularized Sweden, for example, a pastor may have 50,000 baptized persons in his parish and only 50 in the pews. As a kind of public servant he is charged with the onerous task of keeping the vital statistics and records of all in his parish. As a Christian pastor, with excellent theological education, he knows what the Gospel is and what the Church is intended to be. But he is overwhelmed by the numbers and the indifference and unbelief of his parishioners. So it may relieve his anguished sense of vocational frustration to know that his liturgical ministrations are somehow performed, with prayers, on behalf of the missing thousands. Likewise in England, the British Congregationalist, Sydney Cave, once observed without rancour that one result of the liturgical movement within the Church of England was that fewer and fewer persons were attending more and more sung Eucharists. But these unfortunate aberrations in lands which have been dismally afflicted by defection from the faith do not prove that Holy Communion, when frequently celebrated, is a flight from reality. On the contrary, the main current of contemporary theological thinking about the meaning of worship insists that the Church's worship, especially the Holy Communion, is integrally tied in with the witness and social ministrations of the Church. Both the teaching and habit of John Wesley are instructive in this regard. His personal life was even more eloquent than his famous sermon 'On the Duty of Constant Communion'. Accomplishing two or three times as much worthwhile work each day as some of the best of us can do now, Wesley still took time for the Holy Communion on an average of every third day of his long life. Between this frequent Communion and the heroic achievement of the man it is fair to see an effective relation.

It would be pretentious to claim that the daily breaking of bread in Jerusalem established for all time a normative practice of daily participation in the Lord's Supper. But the reflection of many Christians upon the significance of the New Testament example combines with their actual experience of weekly Communion to suggest that this is a frequency which more churches could with profit adopt as their own rule.

To urge this is not to make the mistake of promising an automatic increase of spiritual benefits to all communicants. The danger of the rite's becoming for some people a sacramental motion without meaning is as menacing where Communion is frequent as where it is seldom observed. Furthermore, while the sacrament may rightly be called a means of grace, God's grace must not be thought of as a substance or quantity. The mere multiplying of occasions for receiving the bread and wine does not assure one of a proportionate increase in the reception of grace. For most Christians, however, there is probability that more frequent participation will sustain and strengthen their sense of personal communion with God through the intensified concentration of both mind and will upon God's saving work in Christ.

The restoration of weekly Communion in Methodist, Presbyterian, Baptist and other Protestant churches is not likely to come about very easily or very soon. A ponderous mass of bad liturgical habit, due more to carelessness than conviction, will first have to be changed. And before change can occur in any effectual way, a very large number of pastors, teachers and other congregational leaders must develop an enlarged understanding of the sacrament and deepen their belief in its value and power. For virtually all have sinned and fallen short of an adequate knowledge of the meaning and efficacy of the Lord's Supper in the life of the Church.

So in order to assist in the overcoming of lethargy in this liturgy we take up the second implication of the apostolic devotion to the breaking of bread: our comprehension of its theological meaning.

SEVEN

Six Theses concerning Communion

THE HOLY COMMUNION has been a major factor in every culture dominated by Christians and in the perennial move-ment of the extension of the Church into all the world. Scholars, saints and preachers (including persons qualified to be known by two or three of those names at once) have articulated their wisdom and devotion concerning the blessing and sharing of the bread and the wine, extolling the manifold benefits of eucharistic worship and attempting to interpret its profound and diverse meaning. And regrettably the firm convictions of divided Chris-tians concerning this sacrament have caused an immense amount of strife, inciting polemics and deepening the formidable divi-sions of the Church.

Against the broad background of thought and experience and voluminous writing of Christians through centuries of celebrating the Communion, it seems foolhardy to essay a brief exposition of it. Indeed many Christians feel that they already know enough about the Communion to satisfy their needs. Suggested mean-ings which are not already a part of their understanding may be resented. It is like discoursing on romantic love between man and woman: lovers do not need scholarly, scientific advice. Nor can one man's exposition ever take account of the full range of sacramental theory and meaning. If one visits all the churches from Winesburg to Corpus Christi to Sacramento, he will be amazed to see how time has permitted profuse variations on the theme of the bread and wine and prayers of the earliest rite. In this great diversity of practice and meaning, we can appreciate why the Eastern Orthodox Christians, following the Greek of the New Testament, refer to it as a *mysterion*: it is a divine mystery surpassing all our rational and cognitive capacity.

Yet we need not remain dumb before the mystery. Although all mortal flesh may keep silence in the celebration of it, we can express the results of our reflection upon it. So in the light of biblical teaching, Church tradition and current liturgical thought we are justified in advancing *six theses* concerning the essential meaning of the Holy Communion. These refer to (a) the authority for the sacrament, (b) the presence of Jesus Christ, (c) the symbolic power of both elements and actions, (d) the indissoluble attitudes of remembrance, experience and expectation, (e) personal participation in the Lord's sacrifice, and (f) the communion (*koinonia*) of the saints about the Lord's table. Comments upon each must necessarily be brief, merely suggesting the scope of an adequate discussion.

(a) *Either the Holy Communion is observed in obedience to the will of Jesus Christ, or it is a mere option of the Church.*

Did Jesus explicitly instruct his disciples, and by implication the whole Church, to break bread and drink wine together in His name and memory? An uncritical reader of the King James translation would find an affirmative answer beyond dispute. In Luke 22[19] it says just as plainly as in the carved letters of countless communion tables: 'This do in remembrance of me.' Could anything be more direct and incontestable? That this command is not to be found in the parallel accounts in Mark and Matthew could be explained as simple omission. After all, it stands clearly in Luke as a word of Jesus. Or does it? The *Revised Standard Version* is as distressing on this point as it is for some conservative Christians on the 'young woman', rather than the 'virgin', of Isaiah 7[14]. Following Goodspeed and others, the RSV relegates the command of Jesus to a footnote, explaining that the most ancient and dependable Greek texts simply do not contain these words. The late Dean C. T. Craig supported this reading, saying: 'We can hardly contend that the words came from Jesus.'[1] The familiar words of institution were possibly derived from St Paul's

1. *The Interpreter's Bible* (N.Y.: Abingdon, 1953), X. p. 137.

account in 1 Corinthians 11[24] and added to a later version of Luke's Gospel.

The account given there by Paul is best known to all Christians. It is incorporated in the great prayer of consecration in some liturgies: 'Do this, as often as you drink it, in remembrance of me.' But where did Paul learn these words? He did not invent them. But he said: 'I received from the Lord what I also delivered to you' (11[23]). Where and when? On the road to Damascus, where his apocalyptic meeting with the risen Lord took place? This is neither recorded nor likely. A more plausible answer is suggested by Oscar Cullmann, who proposes that when Paul speaks of receiving from the Lord a certain word, he means that he received the apostolic tradition of the earliest Church, i.e. the witness of those who could trace the word back to Jesus himself.[2] So the problem of the authenticity of both Paul's quotation and Luke's becomes shrouded in the indistinct realm of oral tradition.

If even good, faithful Christian scholars cannot attest to the authenticity of the command to perpetuate this breaking of bread, must the rest of us be resigned to the belief that Jesus Himself did not authorize the Supper we still call the Lord's? By no means! It is still both legitimate and highly important to call this a 'dominical' sacrament, in the sense that the Lord, the dominus, willed it for his followers. We have sufficient basis for thinking that the earliest Christians held unquestioning conviction that their Lord wished them to continue this holy practice. For they knew the apostles who had gathered with Jesus on the night He was betrayed. The story of this Last Supper is told with prominence by all three synoptic evangelists, however their accounts may vary. And the continuance of the tradition in Paul's letter gives further evidence that from the outset this was known to be a practice commanded by Jesus Christ. It is scarcely to be wondered, then, that throughout the centuries of the

2. Essay on 'Tradition' in *The Early Church* (Philadelphia: Westminster, 1956; London: S.C.M., 1956), p. 62.

Church's history, despite sporadic defections, there has been no break in the persistent devotion of Christians to this sacramental act. Indeed, so strong has been the conviction of Christians that the Holy Communion (along with Baptism) derives from Jesus Christ and thus belongs to the very essence of the Church, that almost all the main families of churches—Catholic, Anglican, Lutheran, Reformed, and Methodist—have defined the Church in terms of a faithful community in which the Word is preached and the sacraments administered.

(b) *Either the presence of Jesus Christ is a 'real presence' or he is not the living and present Lord at all.*

Recently in a rather over-dressed Methodist church there was a Communion service being held, during which the excellent choir sang in Latin a fine anthem by Mozart. It was the 'Ave verum corpus', the superb musical adoration of the Blessed Sacrament, which Mozart composed presumably for use in the Salzburg cathedral. The faces of the worshippers were also composed, that is, serene and quite intent. The words of the anthem were printed with translation on the programme for all to see. No one ever uttered a word of objection. But if the minister, instead of the choir, had dared to address himself to the altar in the same 'popish' idiom, his tenure in this lucrative benefice would have been limited indeed!

Somehow the conventional Protestant mind is incapable of separating the notion of the real presence of Jesus Christ from the Roman Catholic dogma of transubstantiation of the elements. It has not been revealed to such mind that the only alternative to a real presence is an unreal presence, which is no presence at all. Some are content to hold this view. To put it candidly and a little rudely, for such Christians the Lord's Supper is something done for the sake of its inspirational values only: it is a significant way of remembering Jesus and His passion, but its meaning is wholly explicable in terms of the worshipper's psychology, glandular secretions, and sense of history. But pious talk of a

divine presence stretches the credulity of the scientific or prag-
matic mind.

Now we need not here engage in a lengthy dispute against the
eucharistic beliefs held by our Roman Catholic friends. Even
though the canons of the Council of Trent pertaining to the
sacrifice of the Mass declare a nine-fold anathema against us for
our disbelief, we must be prepared to stand the consequences.

But the truly Protestant stance is hardly the same as the
cavalier denial of the supernatural presence of the risen Christ
in the action and communion of breaking bread and drinking
wine. For when we draw near with faith and take this holy
sacrament to our comfort, when we hear the Gospel of the death
and resurrection of Jesus Christ, when we acknowledge and
bewail our manifold sins in faith that God through Christ forgives
us, when we offer our sacrifice of praise and thanksgiving and
ourselves in toto to be used of God, and when we eat and drink
the two elements in remembrance that Christ died for us—
in this whole action we know and believe that the ever-living Son
of God is here with us. This is neither a crass conception of His
presence in the elements, which can be handled only by certain
sanctified hands, nor a general idea that the Deity, being immanent, must be here as in every other dimension of human experience. Rather it is a recognition that the eternal Christ in His
mercy has appointed a kind of circumstance, which can be
effected at will by His people, and in which He makes Himself
spiritually present to all who participate faithfully.

And if we are asked how He does this, we are best advised to
admit that it is beyond our rational comprehension and verbal
expression. There is penetrating wisdom in the observation made
by Eastern Orthodox theologians that we Western Christians,
whether Roman Catholic or Anglican or generally Protestant, are
too prone to seek a final explanation for the inexplicable mystery
and holiness of Christ's presence. This penchant for reducing
the ineffable mystery to a set of philosophical propositions has
never been successful as a rational revelation of His presence.

And worse, it has been the source and continuing cause of much mischievous strife among otherwise decent Christians. For four hundred years there has been a grievous running-battle between Lutherans, Calvinists and Zwinglians over the definition of Christ's presence. But after all the bickering over ubiquity and the subtleties about substance, the results have usually been theologically fruitless and detrimental to the health of the Church. The conflicts among Anglo-Saxon churches, while characteristically more restrained and mild than those on the Continent, have hardly been less disruptive of the peace and unity of the Church.

It is heartening, therefore, to discern signs of convergence among the diverse church traditions with respect to the meaning of Christ's presence in the sacrament. In 1954 at the assembly of the World Council of Churches in Evanston, the several Lutheran churches which are members, after considerable wrangling about the grave dangers of illicit 'altar fellowship', decided to hold an open service of Holy Communion. Endeavouring to screen out the ones who might be thought objectionable by their presence, they announced that only baptized Christians who believed our Lord Jesus Christ to be truly present in this sacrament were invited to participate. It was a matter of bewilderment to some and of joy to others when a good number of Presbyterians, Methodists and Congregationalists appeared at the altar. For they too believed! At the next assembly in New Delhi in 1961 the Lutheran invitation was less forbidding still.

A significant step towards agreement on the real presence among Christians of widely diverse background was taken in India in 1955. It has implications not only for Indian churches, however, but for those of at least five great denominational families in the world at large. The Church of South India had been in existence as a multiple union for eight years: Methodists, Presbyterians, Anglicans, and Congregationalists in one undifferentiated body. Desiring to extend the blessings of unity, the CSI had been in theological dialogue with the Lutheran churches, which represent the mission work of American, German and Scandinavian churches. As expected, the Lutherans were cautiously concerned to know what this new ecclesiastical phenomenon understood the Lord's Supper to mean. Papers were read, questions were posed, prejudices were aired and laid to rest, the Scriptures were searched, the Holy Spirit was not quenched. In sum, an agreement was arrived at in a most responsible manner. And the paragraph on the manner of Christ's presence is worthy of wide reception, for it states what a large number of divided Christians have been wanting to say together. It reads:

> The manner of Christ's presence in the bread and wine of the sacrament is a mystery which our minds cannot comprehend, but which we joyfully confess and in which we glory. Though we cannot express this mystery in words, we must, on the one hand, deny that in this sacrament we eat the material flesh of Jesus of Nazareth; on the other hand we must deny that Christ's presence in the sacrament depends upon our faith, or that in it we receive the body and blood of Christ spiritually apart from eating and drinking the bread and wine. We believe that as we receive the bread and wine according to His commandment, we receive the body and blood of Christ in a spiritual manner because of the sacramental union which He has established by His word.[3]

When one reads the formulations of the great confessions of the Protestant churches—the Formula of Concord, the Westminster Confession, the Thirty-nine Articles of the Church of England and John Wesley's reduced version of twenty-five—it is amazing to see how much they have in common in their expression of the spiritual and heavenly manner of Christ's presence and the reception of His body and blood. Perhaps the time is

3. *Agreed Statements*, edited by J. R. Chandran (Madras: Christian Literature Society, 1960), p. 23.

not far off now, when many churches which still adhere to obsolete reasons for keeping a fence around the Lord's Table will discover in their common faith and experience that the one, living, redeeming Lord is truly present to all his people in this solemn and joyful sacrament.

(c) *The efficacy and symbolic power of the Lord's Supper reside both in the elements and in the sacramental action.*

Day after day through the history of mankind marked A.D. millions of lips have phrased the elemental petition: 'Give us this day our daily bread.' In lands of poverty and near-famine, bread or its indigenous equivalent means life's sustenance. No bread, people die! In prosperous lands where the earth's minority are well fed, and where bread is actually as rich as cake, the petition for daily bread is still an appeal for the essential food for living. It is not to be wondered at that in nearly every culture since ancient times the making of bread and breaking of bread have been of elemental significance to man's survival and happiness.

In the practice of the early Church there is good evidence that the symbolism inherent in bread was sufficiently strong to enable this substance to represent the whole import of the Eucharist. In the Acts of the Apostles 2[42] and 20[7] the writer did not feel the need to mention wine as a concomitant in the Christians' rite. Down through the third century the practice of some churches was to use only the bread in the Lord's Supper, while others were content with bread and mere water.[4] But such simplicity eventually changed, as the Christians in effect decided that, with respect to the Holy Communion, man cannot live by bread alone. In the course of time the Western Latin church, disregarding the apostolic teaching of Paul, seemed to regard the wine in the chalice as somehow more sacred than the bread on the paten. Since Christ was believed to be truly present in each element

4. Cf. Hans Lietzmann, *Mass and Lord's Supper*, pp. 195–203.

anyhow, and since there was more danger that the wine might be spilt and so desecrated, only the bread was distributed to the communicants. Against this one-sided Communion was launched the reforming attack of John Huss and the 'Utraquists', who demanded that both bread and wine be given to the people. Huss paid with his life for this conviction. And fortunately the practice of giving 'both kinds' has prevailed in the churches of the Reformation tradition ever since.

A striking feature of the Holy Communion, as seen by the student of religions, is the very commonplace nature of the two materials employed by Jesus in the instituting of it. He did not use words and incantations of an abracadabra sound. He eschewed the exotic ritualism which belonged to the Eleusinian and other mystery religions of his time, and which are reflected today in the initiatory rites of some fraternities and lodges. Instead of these, Jesus chose the simple ritual of the family meal, and as a part of it the two ordinary elements of food and drink. Many cultural anthropologists have been readily disposed to show the analogy between the Christian sacrament and primitive rites of magic. But how stupid it is to compare the symbolic use of bread and wine in the context of solemn prayer with, for example, the witches' cauldron as revoltingly described in *Macbeth*:

> *Eye of newt, and toe of frog,*
> *Wool of bat, and tongue of dog,*
>
> .   .   .
>
> *Liver of blaspheming Jew,*
> *Gall of goat, and slips of yew*
> *Sliver'd in the moon's eclipse,*
> *Nose of Turk, and Tartar's lips.*[5]

No; the consecrated bread and wine are crammed with religious meaning for us precisely because they are not bizarre and exotic, but are entirely familiar and common to mankind. The

5. Act IV, Scene 1.

faith of Christians is in the God who demolishes the distinction between the intrinsically earthy and the sacred by making all things either profane or holy according to their use in the purpose of God.

The contemporary liturgical movement is sending through the churches of many denominations its waves of corrective and salutary influence upon the forms and understanding of worship. Despite its manifest values, however, it tempts some poorly discerning ministers to a distorted and superficial view of liturgy. Some pastors of traditionally Protestant churches, for example, are now prone to be infatuated by the dilettante uses of the so-called sacramentals, before they ever arrive at a sound, theological understanding of what the liturgy is all about. Already one can note the trend away from common bread to either the tiny machine-made biscuits or the paper-like wafers which have Christian symbols stamped upon them, presumably to make them more fitting for holy use. And it is almost amusing to see that, just as some Protestants are falling for this kind of sacramental vogue, the liturgical movement is causing Roman Catholics and Anglicans and certain Lutherans to return to more simplicity and austerity. Referring to this development, the Church of England's Bishop of Woolwich (one of the last survivors of that excellent species, the scholarly theologian-bishop), John A. T. Robinson, writes mordantly of the service as it prevails in his own communion:

> The whole thing reeks of a conception of holiness that is almost the complete opposite of everything for which Christianity stands, a conception of the holy defined in purely Jewish terms, as that which is not common. For our own College Communion at Cambridge, we insisted upon an ordinary loaf baked in the College kitchens and some claret from the College cellars brought up in a good secular decanter by a couple of ordinary undergraduates. Unless the bread and the wine we offer at Communion really comes off the table of

our common lives, out of the midst of our weekday world, then there is nothing for the process of redemption to work on.[6]

In line with this refreshing assertion, it is good to join in the Lord's Supper in the Methodist Church of Switzerland, where that incomparable, crusty Swiss bread is passed from person to person, each breaking off his portion. And it is wholly to be welcomed that in India today a few churches are beginning to use their ordinary flat bread, known as chappati, and which is baked over the coals, instead of an alien importation from the West. And since India is not a wine-growing country, and the State governments have been more effective in enforcing prohibition than a Women's Christian Temperance Union leader would dare dream for America, the price of wine, or even of grape juice, is so high that for financial reasons alone some Christians gladly look for a liquid substitute. In the Punjab, it is reported, a cup of sugared water is used with the broken chappati to be the blood and body of the Lord.

Nevertheless there was a debate among Indian Christians in a conference on the indigenizing of worship, in which the majority declared that it would be a grievous impairment of the Lord's Supper if real wine were forfeited for any reason at all. They felt that this would be a breach of their oneness with churches in all countries. And further, that the symbolism of wine in the Bible is of indispensable worth in worship. In biblical usage, wine in the cup symbolizes two opposite but complementary emotions of man. In the Psalms especially, the cup of wine received from the host was the symbol of joy in life's goodness: the cup overflowed with wine, making glad the heart of man. But conversely, the cup could be one of bitterness. In the narratives of Jesus's passion it was a symbol of his dreadful suffering prior to death. It is evident that in St Paul's thought the latter meaning of suffering was intended where wine was equated with Jesus's blood. Yet Luke reported how Jesus said that he expected to drink the fruit

6. On Being the Church in the World (London: S.C.M., 1960; Philadelphia: Westminster, 1963), p. 67.

of the vine in the coming Kingdom of God; so wine, like bread, was a symbol of consummated life. One cannot look for logical neatness in religious symbolism. And the appropriateness of wine in the Holy Communion is due precisely to the variety and power of its impact upon the mind. As Joseph Sittler captured in a phrase this bitter-sweet ambivalence of the eucharistic wine, it is 'the believer's toast of terrible joy'.[7]

Bread, wine—and an action. There is no sacrament until the bread is distributed and eaten, the wine passed about and drunk, the prayers uttered to God.

Some Protestants shrink reflexively from the word 'liturgy' just as they do from 'Eucharist'. Yet both of these are perfectly suitable derivations from the New Testament Greek. There is no reason at all why they should be treated with the same courtesy which is accorded small-pox, nor be rendered objectionable by the connotations of 'Catholic' or 'high church', as these terms are conventionally used. For the word 'liturgy' is from *leitourgia*, and this in turn is derived, perhaps, from *laos* ('people') and *ergon* ('work'). Liturgy, then, is 'the work of the people of God'.[8] Although in later years it came to refer mainly to the Eucharist, it had the wider range of Christian worship and service within its earlier meaning. In so far as it refers to the Lord's Supper, liturgy means that the people gathered together are not merely absorbing divine grace, like a group of sponges in the rain. They are not present before the table in order to 'commune' aesthetically with a cosy numinosity, but to employ their minds and wills and hands and tongues in an action of praise and thanksgiving.

It is well worth considering the place of active, transitive verbs in the liturgical language of most rituals of the Lord's Supper. So far as these retain the biblical injunctions, they say: *Take* this. *Eat* this. *Drink* this. *Do* this. These actions hearken back to the last meal of Jesus with His disciples. Jesus Himself *broke* the

7. *The Nature of the Unity We Seek*, edited by Paul S. Minear (St Louis: Bethany, 1958), p. 114.
8. The legitimacy of this etymology is questioned, however, by James Barr in *The Semantics of Biblical Language* (London: Oxford Univ. Press, 1962).

bread, took the cup, gave these to His friends and gave thanks to God. So the disciples and first Christians in the Acts of the Apostles 2 broke the bread and distributed food. All such actions were familiar enough to Jesus's followers as Jews. But Jesus gave the actions a new and lasting significance. He commanded them to continue this common custom with a special intention.[9] The act of eating together became enhanced by its inseparable association with God's act in Jesus Christ for the redemption of the world. 'From henceforth the disciples would be bound to associate this act ... with all that His life, and supremely the consummation of that life, mean for them and for all mankind.'[10]

(d) *In the Holy Communion the congregation both remembers Jesus Christ in His life, death and resurrection, and expects Him in the consummated Reign of God.*

It cannot be doubted that a major achievement in liturgical creation in this century is the new Order for the Lord's Supper of the Church of South India. Liturgical scholars as well as plain worshipping Christians have lavished praise upon it. For it is an inspired blending of Eastern and Western traditions, of ancient and modern wording, which somehow succeeds in being original and familiar at the same time. But there is one point at which a more liberal Western Christianity may feel a jolt. It is the congregation's response to the prayer which includes St Paul's version of the words of institution. Repeating a prayer from the ancient Liturgy of St James, the people say: 'Amen. Thy death, O Lord, we commemorate, Thy resurrection we confess, and Thy second coming we await. Glory be to Thee, O Christ.' It is no secret that the idea of 'second coming' raises insurmountable difficulties for many Christians today. We need not take them up here. Nevertheless, there is an essential aspect of the meaning

9. 'It is not that the disciples are commanded to break bread and share wine. . . . It must be, rather, that the command bids them, whenever they do this, to do it *with special intention.*' C. F. D. Moule, *Worship in the New Testament* (London: Lutterworth, 1961; Richmond: John Knox, 1961), p. 33.

10. T. S. Garrett, *The Liturgy of the Church of South India* (Madras: O.U.P., 1954), p. 19.

of the Holy Communion which is preserved in this prayer, but which has dropped out of both the ritual and the faith of some churches. This is the recognition that in the sacramental action both the past of Christ's saving work and the future fulfilment of it converge upon the present moment.

When Suzanne de Dietrich comments on our key passage, the Acts of the Apostles 2⁴², she raises just the right rhetorical question: 'May we not believe that in this simple act of the "breaking of the bread" the early Christians were aware of partaking not only in the Last Supper but also in the resurrection meal? More, of announcing the banquet of the Kingdom? The three events', she concludes, 'were actualized in the gathering of the fellowship.' [11]

Professor Oscar Cullmann with characteristic simplicity writes of the three dimensions as the historical, the contemporary, and the eschatological facts which need to be held together, in terms of the appearance and presence of Christ. 'The Lord appeared to the disciples after His death, while they were eating; He appears now in the cultic meal of the community; He will appear for the Messianic Banquet.' [12]

Having already considered the manner of Christ's presence in the time of celebration, we may look briefly at the implications of our recollection of the Lord as well as our anticipation of him.

When we try to understand the biblical concept of remembrance, we must again sense that frustration of having no English word capable of doing justice to a key word of the Greek Bible. The zealous semanticists of our day make it hard enough to feel confident about the accuracy of speech, even when confined to English. But 'remembrance' is one of those Christian words like 'love', 'fellowship', and 'sacrament', which fails to convey what the biblical Christians wanted to express. The Greek word in question is anámnesis. Generally we can only say, in addition to 'remembrance', that it means a 'memorial' or a 'perpetual

11. *The Witnessing Community*, p. 151.
12. In *Essays on the Lord's Supper* (with F. J. Leenhardt), p. 13.

memory'. Such a concept is conveniently attributed to Huldrich Zwingli, the reformer of Zürich, who is popularly thought to have regarded the Lord's Supper as a 'mere memorial' and nothing more. But this stereotype is as unfair to Zwingli as it is misleading to current thought about the Communion, and as it is inaccurate as a translation of *anámnesis*.

What we urgently need but cannot seem to find or fabricate is a pronounceable word which means the transcending of time in both directions, so that the experience of the worshipping congregation is truly one of participating in the death and resurrection and expectation of the Lord. The German *Vergegenwärtigung* comes close, but is of no use in English-speaking lands. The temporal distance between St Paul and the last earthly days of Jesus was relatively short, just a few years, as compared to the nearly two millennia which separate us from that time. And yet the meaning of *anámnesis* is the same for us as for the apostle. Writing in Greek as a Jewish thinker, Paul could use *anámnesis* to mean 'the restoration of a past situation which has for the moment disappeared', but which 'to remember is to make present and actual'.[13]

But just what is made present by remembrance? Not merely the teachings of Jesus, for these abide in tradition and text. Not a sense of knowing Jesus in the flesh, since this is quite impossible for us. What we have in remembrance, rather, is the whole redemptive action of God in His Son-made-man. In liturgical language, we recollect His 'precious death and passion, and glorious resurrection and ascension',[14] which is to say, the essentials of the apostolic preaching and teaching.

The Communion is therefore a proclamation or announcement of the Gospel, even as preaching is. This is its present relevance for the Church and the world, even though we often allow it to be smothered over with much liturgical pietism. The basic structure of most rituals is intended to provide for a re-

13. F. J. Leenhardt, op. cit., p. 61.
14. From the Order for the Lord's Supper of the Church of South India.

hearsal of the salient moments of the Gospel story. That is why the preached Word ought not to be omitted from any Communion service unless for a special reason. And why should preachers usually offer their people a so-called 'Communion meditation' instead of a straightforward sermon setting forth some basic aspect of the Gospel? For the Holy Communion, like its antecedent, Baptism, is simply the Word made visible, tangible and edible. 'For as often as you eat this bread and drink the cup,' wrote the Apostle, 'you proclaim the Lord's death until he comes' (1 Cor 11[26]).

Until He comes! The conscious omission of this very idea by certain revisers of church rituals, such as the Methodist, speaks in silent eloquence of the desire of many Christians to ignore or reject the future and eschatological reference of the Lord's Supper. This amounts to a rejection of the New Testament concept of hope as well. Being revolted by the apocalyptic imagery of a few passages of the New Testament and of the faith of the Adventists and fanatics, such Christians have tacitly conceded that history has no meaning and no end, and that the Reign of God may be dutifully prayed for but never seriously expected. So the Communion becomes, in this view, a moment of looking back to Jesus with sentimentality and of introspective thoughts about one's personal relation to God. Without the forward prospect, it fails to be an event of thanksgiving and jubilation for the deeds and promises of God.

On the treatment of this question in the New Testament, C. H. Dodd observed: 'As the too crude and literal expectation of the Advent [of Jesus] faded, the Sacrament became the repository of all that proved permanent in the eschatology of the primitive church.' [15] There is no valid reason why the persistence of crude and literal notions held by some Christians in the present day should require us to cease being the community of faithful expectation.

15. *Christian Worship*, edited by N. Micklem, p. 78.

*(e) In the Holy Communion our present self-offering is joined
to the final and unique sacrifice of Jesus Christ.*

It is both a blessing and a penalty for Christianity that it grew
out of the Hebrew tradition. The blessing is clearly seen in the
monotheism, ethical fibre, and insight into God's saving work in
history which we derive from ancient Israel. But the penalty lies
partly in the fact that Gentile Christians, and especially
twentieth-century Americans and Europeans, find it virtually
impossible to have full understanding of the New Testament
language about the sacrificial death of Jesus. We are forced to
deal with an idiom which is completely foreign to our minds.
And if the experts, the biblical and liturgical scholars, get tied
into such intellectual knots as they do when trying to explain the
meaning of blood-sacrifice, atonement and covenant, what shall
the rest of us think?

To discuss the Eucharistic sacrifice in negative terms is easy
enough. Whatever else may divide Protestant churches, they are
at one in their common rejection of the sacrifice of the Mass, as
believed and interpreted by the Roman Catholic Church. But
we cannot worship simply according to the power of negative
thinking.

In a positive way, but without elaboration, we can affirm certain beliefs about the sacrifice. First, there is no doubt that the
Jewish metaphors pertaining to animal sacrifice are applicable in
all reverence to Jesus's willing surrender to death on behalf of
sinful mankind. Even as the Suffering Servant of Isaiah 53 was
likened to the lamb before its shearers, so the One who fulfilled
the role of the Suffering Servant was instinctively compared by
His followers to the innocent lamb of God. 'For Christ, our
paschal lamb, has been sacrificed' (1 Cor 5⁷). All four Gospels
present His death as an offering for atonement. And the Letter
to the Hebrews, with its detailed description of Christ's priestly
office, makes the sacrificial language fairly intelligible to the
modern reader. But note that Hebrews does not relate Christ's

death to the Lord's Supper, nor even in 10^{29} and 13^{10} make a veiled reference to the Supper.

The second affirmation, therefore, is that the sacrifice of Jesus Christ is absolutely unrepeatable. Four times the point is hammered down in *Hebrews* that His death and sacrifices were 'once for all' (7^{27}, $9^{12,\ 26}$, 10^{12}). If this most priestly book of the New Testament so clearly rejects the notion of a repetition, and if it has no warrant in other books, how can the Roman dogma be regarded as anything but unbiblical, and even anti-biblical?

Thirdly, by the merits and death of Jesus Christ, and through faith in His blood, we and the whole Church receive remission of our sins, and all other benefits of His passion. While the death of our Lord was once for all, the effects of His whole act of self-oblation are perennial and universal. Because of this we have the assurance of forgiveness. In Christ's self-giving we have a new covenant with God, in which He has both laid His obligations upon us and given us the promise of redemption.

Therefore, in the fourth place, we can speak unambiguously of the sacrifice of ourselves for God's service, and the joining of this personal sacrifice to the unique self-offering of Jesus Christ. We do this, not as individuals only, but as the corporate community, the Body of Christ. True to the New Testament description of our vocation as Christians, we are a corporate priesthood. Thus in the *Hymns on the Lord's Supper*, Wesley dared to use this sacrificial language:

> Ye royal priests of Jesus, rise,
> And join the daily sacrifice;
> Join all believers, in His name
> To offer up the spotless Lamb.[16]

Not only our praise and thanksgiving, but our offering of money, the bread and wine and all the labour and commerce they

16. *Poetical Works of John and Charles Wesley*, Vol. III (London, 1896), No. 137, p. 319; quoted by John C. Bowmer, *The Sacrament of the Lord's Supper in Early Methodism* (London: Dacre, 1951), p. 183.

represent, and every other aspect of our personal being and living we offer up through Christ to the God of glory.

(f) Our communion, or koinonia, with the Lord and with our brethren finds both its impetus and its clearest expression in the Lord's Supper.

Whenever I either administer or receive the eucharistic elements, there are two phrases from two ancient languages which inevitably come to mind. One is from the Orthodox Liturgy: *Ta hagia tois hagiois*. It means: 'The Holy things unto them that are holy.' The other is derived from the disputation over the meaning of the Lord's Supper in Luther's time, especially at Wittenberg in 1536: *manducatio impiorum*. This means that the bread is eaten by the unworthy. Putting these two phrases together, we find an apt designation of the Communion. It is the supper of the sinful saints. The holy people of God, called to be saints in His service, are yet the community of forgiven sinners. So at the Communion we sense both the depth of our unworthiness and the joy of being joined in fellowship with the holy God. Here the communion of saints becomes an experienced reality. As the forgiven ones we can worship in company with the whole Church in heaven and on earth.

It is because of this awareness of being members of the worshipping community that all merely individualistic feelings are a threat to the integrity of the Communion service. Indeed the kind of individualistic piety which is actually encouraged in many churches is a deplorable distortion of the purpose of the sacrament. Already the common chalice has been surrendered in the interests of social hygiene. (Although Gordon Rupp pertinently asks whether the mortality rate is higher among Episcopalians who use it than among others who use tiny glasses!)[17] Moreover, in many churches, and even in those which normally choose their hymns with care and taste, it is still the practice for the choir to croon softly the songs of self-centred piousness during the time

17. *The Holy Communion* (London: S.C.M., 1947), p. 122.

of the Communion. Worst of all, it seems, is the practice which has a certain currency in America which can most aptly be called 'cafeteria Communion'. Here the bread and the little glasses are simply laid out on the altar rail for anyone to take as he pleases. Not only does this eliminate the role of the minister, since he does not even handle the elements and his speaking part could just as well be played by a tape recorder, it also shatters the concept of corporateness in the Church. It encourages the people to come forward from their pews as atomistic worshippers, oblivious to the presence of their brethren. Although most remote from the Roman Mass in its main respects, this sacramental travesty comes very close to the individualism which actually existed in the congregations of Medieval Catholicism. And in this technological era one can foresee the final outcome of this trend in the form of a eucharistic vending-machine: Bread and wine for a dime!

Since we live not only in an atomic age but also in an atomistic one, it is hard enough in modern society to maintain personal community without adding to that difficulty by the forfeiture of the essential bond of Christian koinonia. If we keep losing ground in the Lord's Supper, we lose in a most significant place. St Paul spoke for all time when he wrote to the church at Corinth that the drinking of the cup and the breaking of bread are our koinonia in the body and blood of Christ, our participation in His life. But he added: 'Because there is one loaf, we who are many are one body, for we all partake of the same loaf' (1 Cor 10[17]). The Holy Communion does not merely presuppose a true community of believers. It is used by the Lord to build up such community.

One of the words spoken by Jesus which is most pertinent to the Communion is this: 'So if you are offering your gift at the altar, and there remember that your brother has something against you, leave your gift there before the altar and go; first be reconciled to your brother, and then come and offer your gift' (Mt 5[23-4]). There are few injunctions of Jesus which are more frequently disregarded than this one. And there are few churches which any longer dare to have the salutary disciplinary rule found in some of the Anglican Churches' constitutions: e.g. 'If the Parish Priest have reason to believe that persons who are parties in a malicious quarrel are likely to present themselves for Communion, he shall warn them and not suffer them to be partakers of the Lord's Table until he knows them to be reconciled.' [18] The grave seriousness of Christian love and forgiveness as well as the integrity of the Communion service as a bond of community could be more effectively taught and manifested if such a rule were obeyed in each congregation.

The problem of broken relations between Christians and the effect of breaking bread was dramatically illustrated in Nashville in 1960 during the 'sit-in' demonstrations. Desegregation of eating places was the goal. One night the home of the city's leading Negro lawyer was bombed. Two thousand students, Negro and white together, marched in silent protest to the city hall. The mayor met them there and cautioned prudence. Indicating their leader, a young minister, he appealed to the fact that they were Christians. 'Let us pray together,' he urged. Whereupon a voice from the crowd called: 'If you can pray together, why not eat together?' He may not have been thinking of the Communion as such, but of common eating. But the issue is the same so far as reconciliation in Christ is concerned.

A liturgical sign of this state of reconciliation in ancient times was the 'kiss of peace'. This has fallen out of use for obvious reasons, as well as for ones not so obvious, such as the fairly recent desegregation of men and women in common worship. But it persists as a ritual action on the part of the clergy in certain churches. Most recently and dramatically it has been restored to Protestant worship in the liturgy of the Church of South India. Only now it is a clasping of the hands, rather than a kiss, which is the sign of reconciliation and peace in the congregation. This

18. *Book of Common Prayer of the Church of India, Pakistan, Burma and Ceylon* (Madras: S.P.C.K., 1961), p. 394.

sign is passed from person to person throughout the church before all proceed to the Communion.

Perhaps the most incisive statement ever made about the meaning of the Lord's Supper for human community within the Church is the admonition of 1 Corinthians 11²⁸⁻⁹: 'Let a man examine himself, and so eat of the bread and drink of the cup. For any one who eats and drinks without discerning the body eats and drinks judgement upon himself.' What does it mean to discern the body? The 'body' is Jesus Christ, the living Lord, who makes himself spiritually present. The 'body' is also the community of faithful persons which is gathered for worship. The failure of any Christian to discern this reality in the eucharistic service spells the deterioration of that person's life in Christ. But the true discerning of the corporate life of the community of Christ is the apprehending of God's grace for the effecting of continued life in the Church, which is His body.

'. . . and the prayers.'

EIGHT

Persisting in Prayer

S O UNIVERSAL among human beings is the practice of praying that we are not in the least astonished to find it cited as one of the four apostolic criteria for the Church. In Christianity, as in every religion from the primitive to the advanced, prayer is taken for granted. It belongs to religion almost by definition. Who can imagine religion without prayer? Without it a Church makes as much sense as an orchestra unable to play music. So is it not enough here to record that Christians pray, and be done with the matter? Not quite! For prayer is an act with distinct content and quality in it. While the majority of men and women do pray with varying degrees of frequency, their acts and thoughts have widely differing meanings. The phenomenon of praying may be almost universal, but the content and intent are by no means uniform among all religions. In fact, between the ways of prayer in some religions and those in Christianity virtually no comparison is possible.

In Jerusalem the earliest Christians persisted in prayer with the apostles. As it was the custom of Jesus to pray in both the synagogue in Nazareth and the great temple in Jerusalem, so the Christians at first saw no need to find an alternative to his practice. Even if they wanted to, they could not suppress the desire to address God, to praise Him and beseech Him for grace and mercy. This was so especially because their new faith was in Jesus Christ, who had given them the highest example, the clearest pattern, and the boldest promise of prayer. Moreover, as years went by, Christians discovered new and unique dimensions of prayer, scarcely known to others. They found by experience the essentially corporate nature of it, praying together as a community of faith rather than just as religious individuals. They found deeper reality in prayer because it was offered in the name of Jesus Christ; that is, their prayer was informed by all they knew of God's self-revelation in their Lord.

We have noticed earlier the tendency unjustifiably to consider the Church of the Acts of the Apostles 2 as a kind of lost Utopia to which Christians look back in longing. Perhaps St Luke as a writer of the history indulged that penchant himself. But there is no good reason to suppose that the first Christians were super-human in their spiritual discipline nor that they possessed innate powers of communion with God which are denied to us. They seemed to have had ample time for gainful employment, missionary witness, as well as a fair share of quarrelling among themselves. Nevertheless we can take at face value the declaration that they devoted themselves to prayer; and the manner and zeal of their prayer were such as to constitute the criterion for us today. Making all due allowances for human faults and frailties in the earliest Christians, we still can see that in comparison to their manner of persisting in prayer, the practice of our present congregations is grossly deficient.

Any person with a fairly critical mind who has attended church services even occasionally can detect the emptiness of much verbal expression which is called prayer. That which is presumed to express the Church's holiness often merely exposes its hollowness. The vacuity of prayer in many churches today has given one writer of paper-back novels an excuse for publishing a deadly caricature of worship as it might be in the year 1993. Entering a church, one hears a whirring noise high above him and asks his guide what it is. 'That's our Praisegod Machine. . . . Actual recordings of the entire congregation. . . . We had a top script man do it up for us. . . . Get this. We had the whole thing multiple-recorded, every single voice multiplied fifty times. . . . We play it all the time. . . . The statistics on it are pretty wonderful. Actually praisewise we figure forty-eight hours of this equals the entire congregation singing away every Sunday for fifteen years!' The visitor, impressed, ventures to say: 'That should make God very happy, all right.' The guide nods smilingly and adds: 'We beam it straight up.' [1] Between the origin of the whirring prayer-wheels in Buddhist temples and the automation of worship in the liturgical fiction just described are two thousand years of human history. But they share the identical error in men's minds concerning the nature of prayer.

The difference between mechanical and personal prayer is perfectly obvious. But less clearly perceived by Christians is the primacy of corporate prayer over individualistic prayer. Despite much justifiable insistence in recent years that radical individualism has little place in the Christian faith, especially in worship, its roots have gone down so deep in Protestant soil that the truly communal worship in a church is gravely impaired. In too many prayers and too many hymns the first person singular crowds out the corporate 'we' of the people of God. It is an interesting and useful exercise at times in public worship, as one is joining in a first-person singular hymn, to transpose the pronouns to the plural: 'Spirit of God, descend upon our hearts,' or 'Our faith looks up to Thee.' Conversely one can sense what is wrong with individualism by turning plural hymns into singular ones: 'A mighty fortress is my God,' or 'O God, my help in ages past.' The rule is not hard and fast, of course; the community does not blot out the individual. Nor is an impersonal collectivism the alternative to individualism. But the community gathers the faithful individual and his personal concerns into the life of koinonia which, as we have seen, is of the very genius of the Church.

Again to quote T. S. Eliot on the corporate quality of the Christian life: 'There is no life that is not lived in community, and no community not lived in praise of God.' Then he defends this thesis by pointing out that even the desert monk in his cave, seemingly the pure form of the solitary man, prays for the Church, the Body of Christ, of which he is a member. How correct is Mr Eliot? Many literary critics have been unable to understand him

1. Shepherd Mead, *The Big Ball of Wax* (N.Y.: Ballantine, 1954), p. 52.

because they do not know how to make anything of his authentic Christian faith. But in this poetic expression on prayer in the Body of Christ is it simply his Anglo-Catholicism showing through? More accurately, it is the New Testament faith being revealed in the poem. It is the basic conviction of all those who through faith have found the meaning of life to be 'in Christ', that is, in the living community of the new humanity which Christ is fashioning in this world on the basis of his redeeming work.

In a clumsy but expressive phrase, Karl Barth frequently refers to the Church as 'the earthly-historical form of existence' of Jesus Christ. If we will know Christ, therefore, we know Him in this corporate form of existence. And if we Christians wish to pray, as we ought, we do so as members of this community. We are plural Christians who worship in the one Body because the one Lord has given Himself for us who are many.

Another expression of this same faith is the practice of praying 'through Christ' or 'in the name of Christ'. This has become a mere habit for many Christians, the perfunctory use of a liturgical formula, suggesting as little real meaning as the word 'love' at the end of a telegram. Yet the whole justification and rationale for Christian worship is implicit in that phrase, 'through Christ Jesus our Lord', or its equivalent. Too easily we forget that our worship of the Almighty God is made possible by our faith in the Son Jesus Christ. Whatever textual problems pertain to Luke 10[22]— that prayer of Jesus which seems to belong more to John than to Luke—there is basic and abiding theological truth in the assertion that 'no one knows . . . who the Father is except the Son and anyone to whom the Son chooses to reveal him'.

We are not as Christians empowered to judge what God thinks of the prayers which are offered by those countless millions of worshippers who have never known Jesus Christ. That is a matter which is staggering to the human intellect and belongs to the omniscience of God only. But we are none the less emboldened to say that, in spite of the claims of other religions, our knowledge of God as Lord and Redeemer is only through Jesus Christ. And once having come to know God through His Son, we cannot offer prayer and worship in any other name. It was through Jesus Christ that God once condescended to our mortal estate in a downward movement of love and redemptive grace; and it is through the living Christ that we respond in faith with the up-ward movement of our self-offering and supplication. As William Nicholls properly expresses this biblical concept of worship, Christ is the true and constant Jacob's Ladder, providing the possibility of communication between God and ourselves.[2]

The corporateness of Christian prayer is determined, then, by the fact that Christ Himself, through whom we know God at all, constitutes us as members of His community. 'All prayer is prayer offered in the Body of Christ,' writes Daniel T. Jenkins, 'and even prayer offered concerning things which appertain to a particular member and to him alone must be offered in the context of the life of the Body and with an eye to the well-being of the whole Body.'[3]

If it may be accepted that all Christian prayer is essentially corporate, we move on to the question of how the communal character of prayer ought to be expressed. If a church can realize its true nature and calling only as it devotes itself to prayer, are there certain irreducible dimensions of worship which must not be neglected? The question implies an affirmative answer. But this affirmation does not in any sense mean that there must be uniformity of prayer and worship in the many churches. The apostolic criterion signifies primarily the persistence in Christian prayers. It does not imply that all must pray alike. Far from it! One of the most widespread and tenaciously held misconceptions about the present movement towards church unity is precisely the fear that all congregations in a united church would be forced to worship according to one form only. It needs to be said again

2. *Jacob's Ladder: the Meaning of Worship* (London: Lutterworth, 1958; Richmond: John Knox, 1958), p. 31. Cf. John 1[51] for this analogy.
3. *Prayer and the Service of God* (London: Faber, 1944), pp. 82-3.

and again that this need not be so. Not only is a wide range of liturgical variation permissible in the united church; it is desirable and valuable to maintain it, simply because Christian people, like other human beings, are not uniform in mentality and sensibility. The familiar debate over the question of whether prayers should be 'set' or 'free' is usually a sterile one. It calls forth the defensive attitude and dogmatism of Christians whose experience is narrow and prejudice fixed. Obviously there are some virtues in both forms, and these are complementary The same may be said of other contrasting forms of liturgical expression: hymns, postures, actions, words. The plain fact that diversities exist within present denominations without breaking their unity ought to lay to rest the fear of uniformity.

Granting the legitimacy and value of diversities of form and expression, what are some of the fundamental considerations in respect to the corporate practice of prayer in the churches?

(a) Observing the behaviour of many Christians, including ministers, in a church, one is led to assert that the first need is to learn afresh that the gathering of a congregation for worship on Sunday morning, or another time, is primarily for the purpose of prayer. It may seem a platitude, or even a tautology, to say this. But the widespread dissipation of earnestness with regard to prayer in public worship poses a problem of churches which is gravely critical.

A few years ago a church magazine sponsored an essay contest, assigning the topic: 'Why I attend church.' In announcing the terms of it, the editors proposed two alternatives: either to enjoy the candle-lit atmosphere of worship, enhanced by whatever architectural props and lighting; or else to hear the preacher's sermon. No third choice given! Not even a hint that the worship of God in prayer might be a valid alternative—much less the primary reason! How representative of prevailing opinion is this?

Certainly we should not detract from the preaching of the Word, both as proclamation and instruction, nor from the reading of the Holy Scripture, nor from any other element of the setting and action of worship which directs men's minds to God. But there is good reason, rather than mere tradition, why the services in some denominations are called simply 'Morning Prayer' and 'Evening Prayer'. And it is not a mere courtesy to the Almighty which is expected of every member in many churches that upon entering the sanctuary he will do nothing else before he has stood or knelt to offer a prayer of thanksgiving to the Lord of the house of worship. Little mottoes about the beauty of silence, or polite invitations to meditate, printed at the top of the morning's bulletin, will hardly suffice to direct people away from the bad habits of clucking, gossiping, or wool-gathering. But a strong and clear interpretation of the awesome purpose of worship can do this, especially as far as young persons and new members are concerned.

The good effects of a trained sense of reverence in church members will be to no avail, however, if there is inadequate provision made for the personal, faithful and intelligent participation of the whole congregation in acts of worship. Whatever the liturgical crudities or emotional excesses of many so-called 'sects' of the land, with their whooping and shouting and reverberating 'Amens', they at least do not suffer from the kind of congregational apathy and aphasia which are now too familiar in some churches. And even while the churches of the Pentecostal and Holiness types are taking some cautious measures to introduce form and dignity in their worship, their opposite in the Catholic tradition are endeavouring to bring the people into real participation again. The familiar slogan of the Catholic liturgical revival is 'Pray the Mass'—meaning that Catholics should cease being either atoms at prayer in the pew or bored spectators of the drama enacted by the priest and his servers at the altar. Already there is a notable resurgence of Roman Catholic congregational life as a result of this integration of priest and people in the liturgy. How much more vitality might be expected in the churches of the Protestant tradition if the members accept not only their share in the active programme of the church but in the regular corporate prayer life as well!

No revolutionary suggestions are here proposed for the achieving of the one great hour of sharing in the fullness of worship each Sunday. Not a clutching after novelty, but effective employing of what is already known is recommended. For example, litanies and unison prayers are certainly worthwhile. They keep the minds of the people intent upon the content of the prayers being offered; and because they require the speaking with one voice they afford the likelihood that the people will pray with one accord.

There is one small word which carries great meaning for Christian worship. It is 'Amen', meaning strong affirmation of the prayer just offered. Few words, if any, have been used so universally and without much alteration in many languages.[4] Now it is sheer nonsense to regard the congregational 'Amen' as a high-church device, as some do. It has the best scriptural warrant as well as a long tradition of Protestant usage. In his perennially helpful book on prayer, George A. Buttrick, though certainly not regarded as a high-churchman, urges the use of the 'Amen' as of much value to the congregation at prayer.[5] It gives audible evidence that members of the congregation are really listening to the prayer spoken on their behalf by the pastor, and that they are alert to the cue he gives for them to make it their own personal prayer by exclaiming 'So be it!'

Likewise the regular use of responsive, or antiphonal, readings of selections from the Bible engages the participation of all members. This is familiar enough in many churches as a kind of dialogue between the minister and the people. But there is a spreading practice of having the alternate portions of the passage read by two sections of the congregation, the left and the right.

4. Cf. the discussion of its biblical usage by C. F. D. Moule, *Worship in the New Testament* (London: Lutterworth, 1961: Richmond, John Knox, 1961), pp. 73–4.   5. *Prayer* (N.Y.: Abingdon-Cokesbury, 1942), p. 286.

This has the added value of giving balance in volume and emphasis to every part that is read; and it fortunately diminishes the contrast between pastor and people.

Finally, the distinctive contribution of the Society of Friends is justly finding wider currency in the churches: the period of thoughtful, expectant silence. It scarcely needs to be explained that the time we live in is one of increasing noisiness and distraction, so there is a psychological value to silence wherever it can be found. But there is spiritual and liturgical value as well. It has been found by experience in corporate worship that deep silence in church makes possible a sense of communion with God and the brethren which can rarely be known otherwise. It is stretching a good thing to call this the 'sacrament of silence', as some do. Silence may serve the purpose of sacrament, or it may be sheer emptiness of mind. Most Christians who are mentally undisciplined for prayer cannot avoid vagaries of the mind during silence. This presupposes a congregation of intensely devoted persons. Even then we cannot claim for silence the same dominical warrant and conformity to the definition of sacrament as for Baptism and Holy Communion. But its liturgical value is none the less significant—if an extended period of minutes, rather than a few token seconds, be allowed. For as Paul Tillich rightly observes, when silence is really silent prayer, it may be the realization of St Paul's description of the Holy Spirit's intercession—'the sighs which are too deep for words'.[6]

(b) It is manifest that much depends upon the role of the minister as leader and guide in corporate worship. We must reject the idea that any certain liturgy is of such objective integrity and value that it only needs to be mumbled on schedule in order to please the Lord. Likewise we must heartily deny the widespread but unavowed notion that everything depends upon the handsome appearance, tone of voice, and dramatic talent of the man in the chancel. A man need not have the voice of a radio announcer nor the ability of a professional actor in order to fulfil his part as a pastor of the worshipping flock. But at least

6. *The New Being* (N.Y.: Scribner's, 1955; London: S.C.M., 1956), p. 138.

we may expect that he is himself a man of prayer, for whom every word used in the church's service has authentic personal meaning. And further, that he will accept whatever training and discipline are required to make him a craftsman in liturgy, not needing to be ashamed, nor in his shame causing the congregation to feel frustrated and misled.

Thou art without excuse, O pastor, if you use the office of leading worship as an indulgence of your own sense of rhetoric or for parading your self-conscious cleverness. Judging another in this regard incurs the risk of being judged oneself; but a few brief suggestions apply to most of us who are ministers.

Don't talk too much! Keep prayers short in length, however long may be the period of the service allotted for prayers. The people can stay with you better on four or five brief, specific prayers than on one which meanders interminably. Be stingy with adjectives and clichés, but generous with clear diction and relevant ideas. Remember that you are speaking audibly not in order that God might hear you but that you might lead the prayerful thoughts of the church members. So speak for them, not to them. Help them to form their own prayers by the provocative power of your own words. The traditional bidding prayer is still very helpful as a way of suggesting important intentions for prayer and keeping the members' minds moving over the concerns and persons to be offered before God. And withal remember that corporate prayer does not consist of much talking, even when the phrases are subtly compounded of proper liturgical vocabulary. It is genuine only in so far as it is the congregation's faithful response to the great and merciful acts of God in creation, providence and redemption, in reliance upon God's covenant and his promises of steadfast love. Therefore prayers and readings and sermon and hymns constitute a unity of expressed faith.

(c) Christian prayer is distinguished from other speech both because it is directed only to God and because of the faith and mental intention which are indispensable to it.

The underlying faith of prayers, as we have stressed before, is not a general sense of trust in the power of an unknown divinity. It is the apostolic faith in the saving revelation of God in Jesus Christ. This means that Christian prayer, like Christian faith, is unalterably based upon the biblical witness. While Roman Catholics are urged to 'pray the Mass', Protestants should urge in the broader sense that Christians 'pray the faith'. The whole range of biblical faith can be expressed properly in prayer, since prayer is precisely our response to the wholeness of God's dealing with us. As our minds give form to thoughts and words of prayer, we should recall with thankfulness God's act of creating, law-giving, judging in historical events, sending His Son, conceiving the Church, giving the Holy Spirit, and promising the coming of His Reign. In the light of this faith, we are inevitably thrown back to the biblical witness for understanding and guidance, and to some extent for the very language of spoken prayer.

The wide consensus among Christians on the relation between the Bible and worship is so patent that we are the more appalled to hear prayers uttered in public which have little to do with either the thought, faith or language of the Bible. When a strong Protestant like Daniel T. Jenkins declares that 'the Bible is passport, guide and interpreter in the world of prayer', we may nod in easy assent.[7] When a devoted Anglican, such as that indefatigable translator of German theological works, Olive Wyon, asserts that it is very doubtful whether prayer can remain Christian at all if it be divorced from the Bible, we may heed her words with approval.[8] But we might be quite astonished to read in contemporary Roman Catholic books on worship such a statement as the following by the Oratorian, Père Louis Bouyer: 'The first and fundamental condition for any liturgical revival which is truly a revival of piety must be a personal knowledge of the whole Bible and meditation on it.'[9] So far has the main thrust of

7. *Prayer and the Service of God*, p. 79.
8. *The School of Prayer* (London: S.C.M., 1943), p. 75.
9. *Liturgical Piety* (Notre Dame University, 1955), p. 253.

the sixteenth-century Reformation been accepted in the twentieth.

Now the Bible is first of all a majestic testimony to the eternity and omnipotence of God. Increasingly the Israelites of the Old Testament learned that the greatness of Yahweh could not be domesticated nor brought within the range of human understanding. And the fact of the incarnation of the Eternal Logos in the New Testament in no degree lessened that apprehension of God's holiness and infinitude. Sören Kierkegaard may well have devised the phrase, 'the infinite qualitative distinction' between time and eternity, between man and God; but it was prefigured in the Bible. And because of it, our first response to God in prayer is necessarily one of adoration and praise. The miracle of prayer resides in the fact that we who are separated from the Creator by that infinite qualitative difference may nevertheless know God, bow before Him in worship, and communicate with Him in personal prayer.

(d) Some have attempted to demonstrate that there is a given pattern of worship and prayer which is authentically Christian. It may be a coincidence only that the pattern they describe bears very close resemblance to that of the denomination they happen to represent. So far as all sorts of Christians and churches are concerned, it is most doubtful whether anyone can prescribe a *lex orandi*, if this means a rigid order of prayer which alone will please God.

The very nature of the Christian's knowledge of God in Jesus Christ suggests, nevertheless, a certain orderly progression of thoughts in prayer. The order is not immutable, but the elements within it are indispensable. The incalculable weight of experience in prayer over the centuries has fortified the claims of essentiality for the following types of prayer: adoration and thanksgiving, confession of sins, supplication for others and ourselves, and personal commitment through faith. We turn to brief comments on each of these.

(1) *Adoration and thanksgiving.* One of the reasons why the

faith of many Christians these days is shallow and diluted and lacking in gratitude is that they have never been brought to an awareness of the infinite magnitude and holiness of God. Neither in personal faith nor in prayer and corporate worship have they felt the slightest disposition to tremble before the awesome power of the One whom we dare call Father. Such Christians have been cheated when, for example, they have never even heard in worship such a prayer as the *Te Deum* or the *Gloria in excelsis*. These are the types of all such prayers which effectively induce the worshipper to bow down before God in adoring obeisance. 'Thou only art holy, Thou only art the Lord'—since early childhood I have felt an undiminished stirring of the soul upon hearing or saying these words. But why has the dimension of adoration of God never been known by some Christians?

Is this not partly explicable in terms of the language of democracy which is inevitably the idiom of Christians who have never lived under monarchy or despotism? By contrast, the prayers of the Bible were always expressed in the courtly language of absolute monarchy. The king was instituted by God to reign over men, and in some numinous way there was a divine aura about the king's person. Therefore the ascriptions of lordship, sovereignty and omnipotence as used in biblical liturgy carried their original royal connotations. These words form the fabric of most of our traditional liturgy as well as the treasury of Christian prayers.

Despite the increasingly egalitarian society of Great Britain, the monarchical language of the Bible and worship still conveys genuine meaning to those subjects of the Queen who are Christians. But what meaning can the words possibly have for democratic—or even republican—Americans? Like the locusts, we have no king. We have an elected president. And during the past three presidential administrations the characteristic forms of address have been these: 'Give 'em hell, Harry! I like Ike! Atta boy, Jack!' Yet the words of our traditional prayers in churches remain appropriate to the mirrored halls of Versailles or the

Court of St James. They would sound silly or insane if addressed to any temporary occupant of the White House.

Having lost the impact of the obsolescent language of adoration, should we not strive diligently to find its equivalent in some other idiom? Without inviting nonsense, it may be suggested that the newly discovered dimensions of space, time, power and knowledge provide the possibility of careful experimentation in language which is both understood by modern minds and appropriate to the sense of wonder which man must always feel when really aware of the presence of God. As the earthly manifestation of nearly absolute power, it is science rather than monarchy which is supreme today. The most apt analogy to divine greatness, therefore, is no longer the royal court but the vastness of space and the unfolding wonders of the whole created universe.

Perhaps an unobtrusive shift from the archaic to the contemporary in language can be effected in the churches by the imaginative and discriminating guidance of pastors and others responsible for public worship. While familiar to older philosophies and sciences, such words as 'cosmic', 'unlimited', 'infinite' have a wide currency and relevance today. Even rather technical terms like 'interstellar' and 'light years' might with care be employed in worship to praise the ineffably holy One who is the Creator of all things.

Another detraction from adoration, apart from language itself, is the disturbing habit into which ministers who frame ex tempore prayers may easily fall. This is the manner of referring to God in the third person when presumably they should be addressing Him in the second person. A prayer begins by being addressed to God as 'Thou'. But soon the minister is asking God that 'the power of God' be given to the people or 'the will of God' be done; or he prays that 'the kingdom of God', rather than 'Thy kingdom', may come. Is this not an awkward way of praying to God? It avoids the direct address which is both respectful and personal. And when prayed by a Protestant, such words imply a purpose much like that of a Roman Catholic praying to a saint, asking St Jude to get something from the Almighty God.

Nor is the matter of posture during prayer irrelevant. With respect to the congregation at prayer it may be argued endlessly whether standing, sitting, or kneeling (what about prostrating?) is to be preferred. Tradition, habit and prejudice against other churches play the determining role in conditioning the posture of most worshippers. But one word about the attitude of both ministers and laymen, as observed in churches, may be to the point here. How can the whole person engage in adoration when the body is sprawled over the pew, arms oustretched for comfort, legs crossed casually? Or the praying pastor, with feet spread apart, hands either in pockets, holding the lectern, or even gesticulating to the Lord! What a contrast to the figure of the young Isaiah, bowing in worship before the Lord in the smoky temple, in the year that King Uzziah died! The body, too, can pray.

(2) *Confession of sin.* It is both theologically and psychologically proper that our prayer of thankful adoration should be followed by confession of sin. The reaction of Isaiah to the overwhelming presence of God is archetypal for us all: 'Woe is me! For I am lost; for I am a man of unclean lips.' It is not a mere matter of tradition, but of our fallen human nature and need of forgiveness, that we should make our humble confession to Almighty God.

Yet there are hundreds of churches today in which the Sunday service includes no prayer of confession at all, even as there is often lack of a prayer of adoration to suggest the need for the confessing of sin. Why confess, when God is not really regarded as the Holy One? Why confess, when the people feel no sense of rebellion or disobedience before God and hence no need of divine forgiveness? How confess, when the minister is too kind or too timid to remind them of their hypocrisy?

Walt Whitman once expressed his envy of the animals because they need never lie awake at night, brooding over their sin. But his envy might just as well be directed towards those Christians today who have inadvertently been allowed to slip into precisely that state of animal existence. For them it is tacitly implied that the gospel of forgiveness through Jesus Christ is really redundant and disposable.

In churches where genuine penitence is neither felt nor expressed, a mood of self-righteousness inevitably prevails. It would almost seem more appropriate for them—at least, more honest—if the familiar prayer of confession were paraphrased like this: 'We acknowledge and declare our manifold acts of goodness, which we from time to time most faithfully have performed by thought, word and deed, provoking most justly Thy pleasure and solicitude toward us . . . etc.' Then in response the minister would need to say no word of absolution, but rather of commendation on behalf of God. Yet Jesus commended the publican, who beat his breast and only muttered: 'God, be merciful to me, a sinner!' (Lk 18¹³).

(3) *Petition and intercession.* Here is the dimension of prayer which properly follows confession and the appeal for forgiveness. It is our appeal to God on behalf of others and in humble supplication for our own basic needs. Probably we are more proficient in praying for ourselves than in other modes of prayer. It is a natural thing for human beings who believe in divine power to seek aid for themselves. In some religions this is all that prayer means: begging for personal satisfaction and the avoidance of misfortune. But Jesus Christ has shown us the full range of prayer's meaning, including both a considerate appeal for sustenance and a loving request for the wellbeing of others. There is a word of his in the Fourth Gospel which is the charter and warrant of all Christian prayer: 'Truly, truly, I say to you, if you ask anything of the Father, he will give it to you in my name' (16²³). But we do not pray as though we confidently believed this promise. If we really trusted in God's offer to us, while making due allowance in our minds for what is appropriate to ask in his name and

what is not, our practice of personal and corporate prayer would be radically revised.

To be sure, there are difficulties for both faith and intellect with regard to petition and intercession. The problems are age-old. How can anything we say or think have an effect upon the working out of God's will? Does God make Himself subject to our wishes? Is His omnipotence not a refutation of the efficacy of man's supplication? Brooding over these issues, some students in a divinity school recently ceased attending chapel services in which intercession was emphasized: they simply could not find theological justification for what they regarded as trying to bend the will of God to their personal desires. They were a strong-minded group, relatively small but unquestionably sincere. Yet one of the finest students in their class, after examining in retrospect all his experiences in the seminary, declared that the intercessory prayers in daily chapel were of the greatest help to his own faith.

Why the difference among students? The latter was as good a theologian as those who doubted prayer's efficacy; he was equally critical and probing in mind. He knew, as did others, that the clay does not tell the Potter what to make. He was also aware of the theological problem of determinism and freedom, of divine causation and human contingency. He was intelligent enough to perceive that the unaccountable wonders of modern science and invention have engendered a widespread popular belief, which turns Tennyson upside down and asserts, in effect, that more things are wrought by dreams than this world prays for! And he knew that all the attractively facile theories about autosuggestion and even telepathy, or extrasensory perception, have little success in providing a hearty rationale for prayer of supplication. But this student knew one more thing, which was apparently not recognized or accepted by the others. It is that, however difficult the theological problem, a Christian cannot really continue in his faith if he does not know the God who hears the prayers of His countless children and acts upon them according to the inscrutable wisdom and love which belong to His perfect will.

Petition is prayed faith. Intercession is prayed love.

Where these are ruled out of practice because of the intellectual difficulties of explaining them, there is a cutting of the nerve of faith in the provident, reconciling and redeeming God.

Often in church services or private worship, however, the omission of intercession for others is not due to any sophisticated intellectual criticism, nor even to a total lack of faith in Christ's promise. Like so many other faults in worship, it is often a matter of sheer carelessness and apathy concerning the relevance of prayer for the needs of persons. The omission from corporate worship often betrays the minister's own lack of awareness of the urgent problems of his people, as well as a deficiency of information about what is happening in the world or even in his own city. The healthy prayer life of a congregation requires direct connection between the periods of intercessory supplication and the clamant needs of persons and groups. The praying pastor must learn of these, obviously, out of his pastoral service, conversations, and the reading of newspapers and church periodicals. Intercession is prayed love for the brethren—but for particular brethren whose particular needs are known. Such prayer ought to be expressed in specific terms, rather than in such meaningless generalities as the appeals for 'blessings for each and every one'. For this dimension of prayer is one of the deepest expressions of the koinonia of the Church as well as of the effectual ministry of the Church to mankind.

Among many possible illustrations of the need for intercession is that for the unity of the Church. This is a prayer which, according to the often cited passage, John 17[21], was offered by Jesus Christ Himself at the time of His passion. In view of the persistent divisions of Christians and churches, it was a prayer of Jesus which apparently has not been answered fully in a positive way. And yet, for this very reason, it is a prayer which we present Christians should feel constrained to continue.

Increasingly we are being driven by both theology and the events affecting the Church in the world to recognize the imperative of Christian unity, and indeed of church unity. And the efforts which are being exerted these days by numerous Christians all over the world for the removal of misunderstanding and prejudice and doctrinal discord are well known. Yet it is a patent insight that, however prodigious and promethean may seem the ecumenical endeavours of our time for the unity of the Church, unity will not be realized unless God Himself uses us for the manifesting of it. Unity is ultimately a matter of grace. It is a divine gift, for it depends upon forms of human reconciliation which God alone is capable of effecting. In this respect, intercession for the unity of the Church is as indispensable as petition for daily bread, or for the doing of God's will and the coming of the Reign.

Despite this urgency, prayers for the reconciling of the divided members, parties and denominations of the Church are offered in relatively few churches. Indeed the whole range of what might be styled 'ecumenical intercession' is neglected. In how many churches is one likely to hear, except on rare occasions, prayers for the manifest unity of the Church? In how many are there earnest and specific intercessions for fellow Christians living in duress, disaster and political persecution? How many diligently pray for the extending mission of the Gospel in the world and for the persons especially committed to it by their vocation? The true but deplorable answer is, not very many. Or how many churches are devoted to praying for sister congregations, for the awakening of those that sleep, for the effective chastening and reform of those which have become complacent, ingrown and pharisaical? For the sick and bereaved, the destitute and suffering, and the anxious and alienated, the god-less and the God-defying?

The entire range of the faith and life of the Church in every land are the proper subjects of petition to God. The whole scope of Christian existence and communal life in the world falls within the realm of intercession. Such prayer is the integral occupation of each Christian congregation. It cannot be satisfied by the feeble tokens of self-centred, semi-distracted, half-doubting, vaguely generalized appeal which we customarily and indifferently bring before the presence of the almighty and most merciful God.

(4) *Commitment*. The prayers of a person, a parson or a congregation are incomplete if they do not include genuine commitment to God. Praise and adoration in themselves are forms of service to God. But they are constantly in danger of becoming vacuous verbiage when unaccompanied by serious intent to serve God in the routine labours and natural struggles of daily living. Unless there is recognizable coherence between protestations to God in prayer and patterns of personal behaviour, something is clearly wrong. Prayer without commitment is like a legal contract without signatures: the right words and concepts are all there, but the element of obligation has yet to be attested.

It is precisely a contract which exists between God and man. It is not a mutual agreement of equals; it is God's gracious assurance and man's promised fidelity. Its seal is the offered life of the Son of God made man. Commitment means primarily the resolve of faithful Christians to live up to their part of the Covenant which God has made with them. Due to the persistence of sin in the life of the redeemed, they may not readily realize this intent in every aspect of living. But it makes a great difference in their relationship to God whether or not they consistently avow their intent to be responsible participants in the Covenant. God's own faithfulness in the 'new agreement' may be taken for granted; it belongs to His nature. Man's may not be. It needs the act of will, which is constantly in tension between faithful obedience and rebellious transgression or careless indifference. But where men by their frailty find it scarcely possible to maintain their part of the Covenant, and yet earnestly desire to keep faithful, it is the grace of God which enables them so to do. 'The Spirit helps us in our weakness' (Rom 8[26]), not only by intercession in our prayers, but by invigorating us to serve the Lord with gladness and fidelity.

This dimension of prayer as commitment is perhaps nowhere expressed so well as in the Covenant service prepared by John Wesley in the eighteenth century. This is without doubt the chief liturgical contribution which Methodism can make to the Church universal. Yet it is strange and deplorable that for several generations this service has been neglected by Methodists, especially in America, until it has been recovered and restored in recent years as a New Year's Eve service. It climaxes significantly in this prayer: 'I am no longer my own, but Thine. Put me to what Thou wilt, rank me with whom Thou wilt; put me to doing, put me to suffering; let me be employed for Thee or laid aside for Thee, exalted for Thee or brought low for Thee; let me be full, let me be empty; let me have all things, let me have nothing; I freely and heartily yield all things to Thy pleasure and disposal. . . . So be it. And the Covenant which I have made on earth, let it be ratified in heaven.'[10]

A prayer of commitment to the Covenant binds an individual Christian to faithfulness in his daily work. A prayer offered by a congregation in this mood of dedication binds it to its task in human society.

While it is quite inadequate to say that the only effect of prayer is the auto-suggestion of the ones praying, it is both true and important that persistence in prayer drives them to actions which are consistent with the goals for which they have prayed. Of course, there is ample space for hypocrisy and self-deception here. Most Christians inevitably fail to live up to the quality of living implied by their prayers. But there is a degree of such failure at which excuses on account of human frailty and moral imperfection become invalid. That point may be as difficult to identify as that indeterminate moment during twilight when day becomes night. But just as we know for sure when night has come, so we can tell when overt defection from God's will makes

10. *The Book of Offices* (London: Methodist Publishing House).

excuses vain. It is then and there that a man or a church body stands judged by the very prayer which has been offered.

Prayer for human brotherhood is a judgement upon a church which excludes persons of certain races or classes from its aloof membership. Prayer for the relief of the hungry, homeless and persecuted condemns the suppliants who give little attention or money to such relief. Appeals to God for economic justice, world peace, and the success of the mission of the Gospel are just a mockery to persons or churches with ingrown minds. Or else— as well it may happen—such prayers, when offered in the spirit of commitment, may sustain the stimulus to the kind of sacrificial, responsible action in the world which is clearly required of us Christians. It is in the context of such prayer that the wholeness of the Church's liturgy, as inclusive of service to God and to the human neighbours, becomes a known reality.

We cannot know exactly how the members of the earliest Christian Church in Jerusalem actually persisted in the prayers. But we may be sure that they regarded prayer, not as an optional indulgence of certain pious ones, but as the indispensable adoration and service of God by the whole community. And it is a fact of importance to the Church as well as the human race itself that never, since the earliest day of the Church's existence, has the corporate prayer of Christians ceased being offered up to God in the name of Jesus Christ. This prayer has sustained the Church in its life and mission through the centuries. This prayer has made the Church susceptible to the new energy and reforming power of the Holy Spirit, despite its frequent retreats from the apostolic faith and defections from its given character. It is through the persistent, fervent, thoughtful and faithful prayer of all Christian people that God's saving purpose for mankind will be fulfilled.

Index of Subjects and Persons